#26

BOY.

MEMORIZE THAT WELL.

...IS THE CREST OF THE EMPIRE WHERE YOU WILL BE RESIDING FROM NOW ON.

THAT SYMBOL...

D0886281

SO THAT'S...

THAT'S RIGHT!

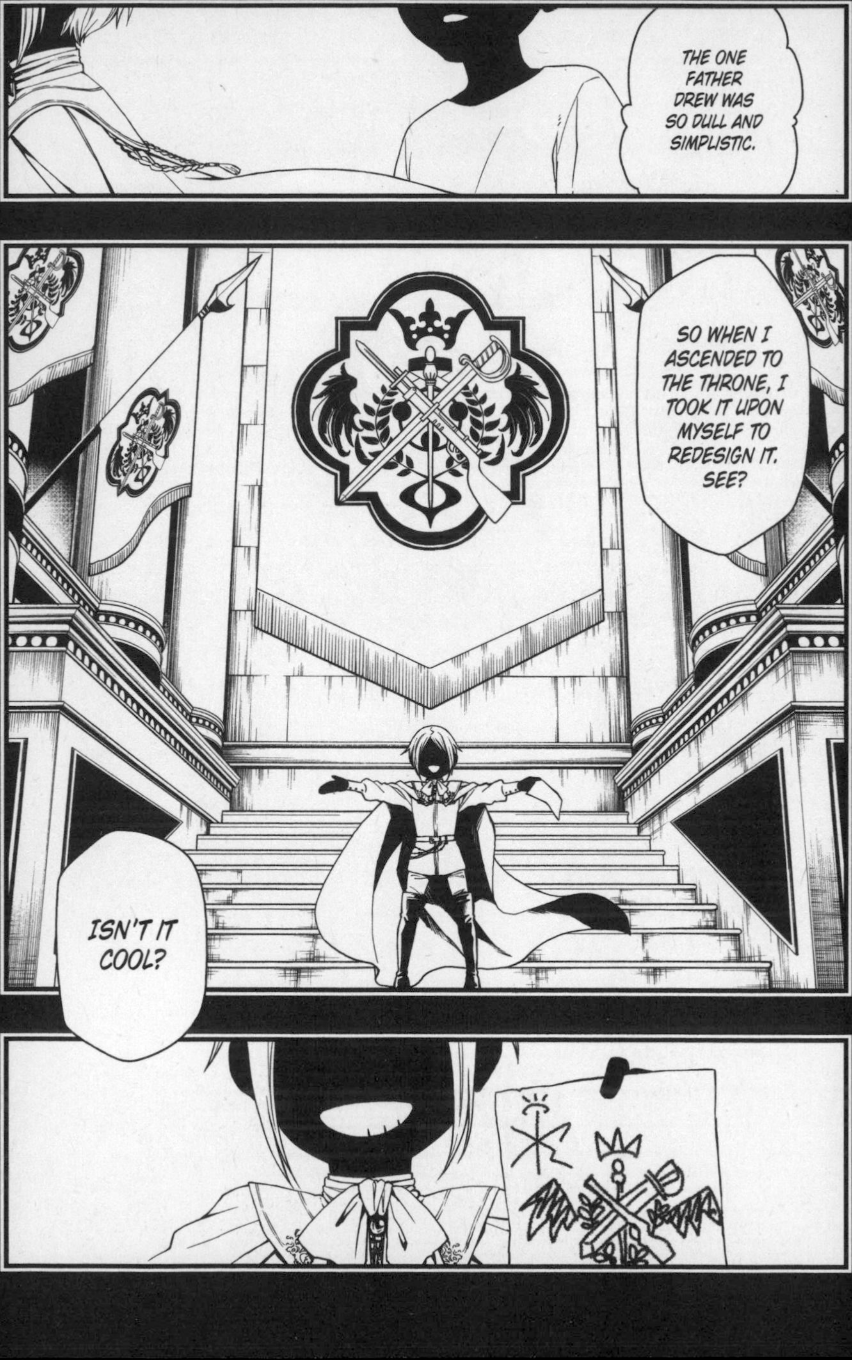
THE ONE FATHER DREW WAS SO DULL AND SIMPLISTIC.
SO WHEN I ASCENDED TO THE THRONE, I TOOK IT UPON MYSELF TO REDESIGN IT. SEE?
ISN'T IT COOL?

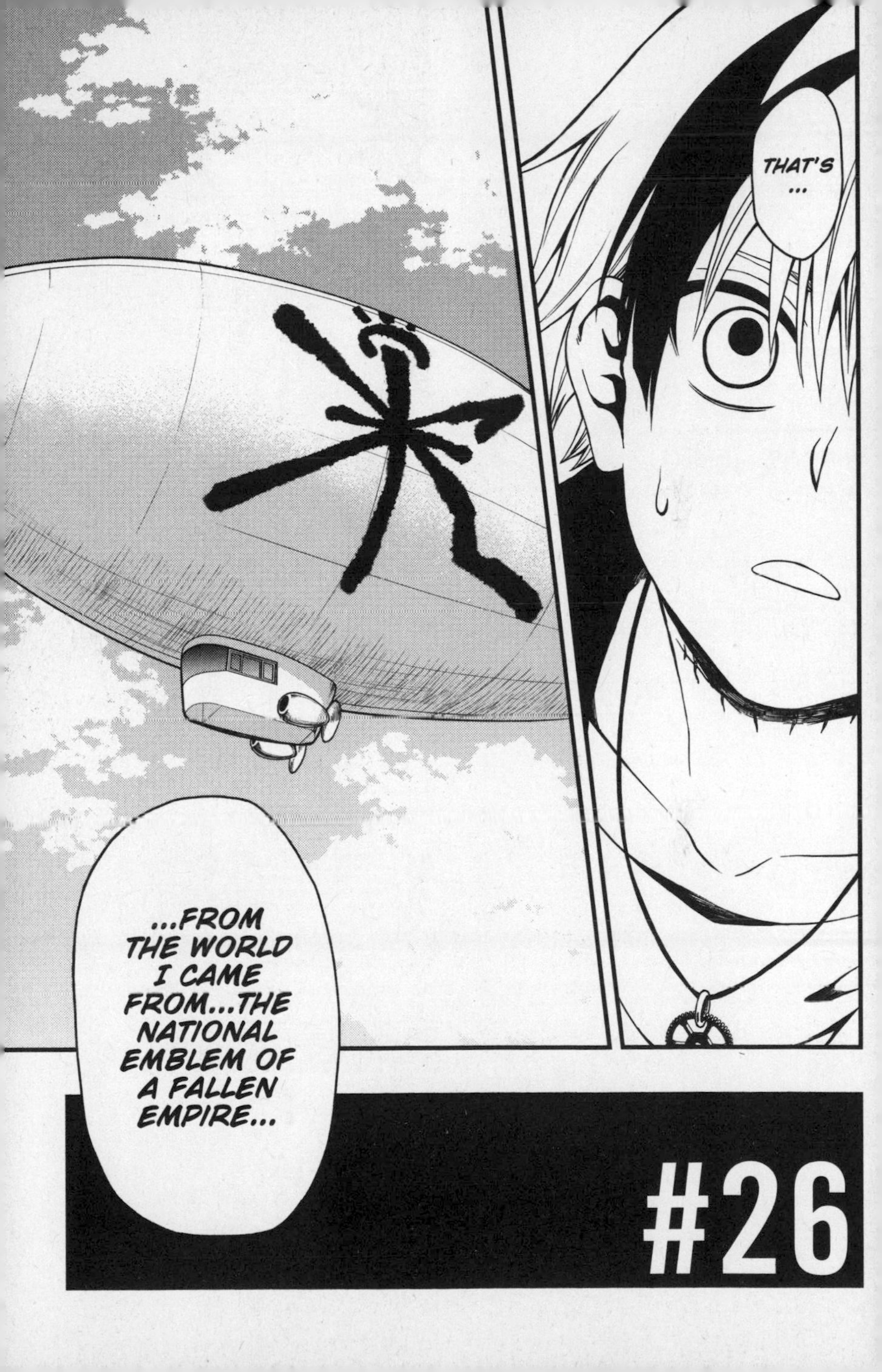
THAT'S ...
...FROM THE WORLD I CAME FROM...THE NATIONAL EMBLEM OF A FALLEN EMPIRE...
#26

It's a dire situation.|

: Why was it revealed?

: Why?

: Where did it leak from?

625s: Where did it leak from?

479z: Another of Bug's associates was burned alive in Japan.

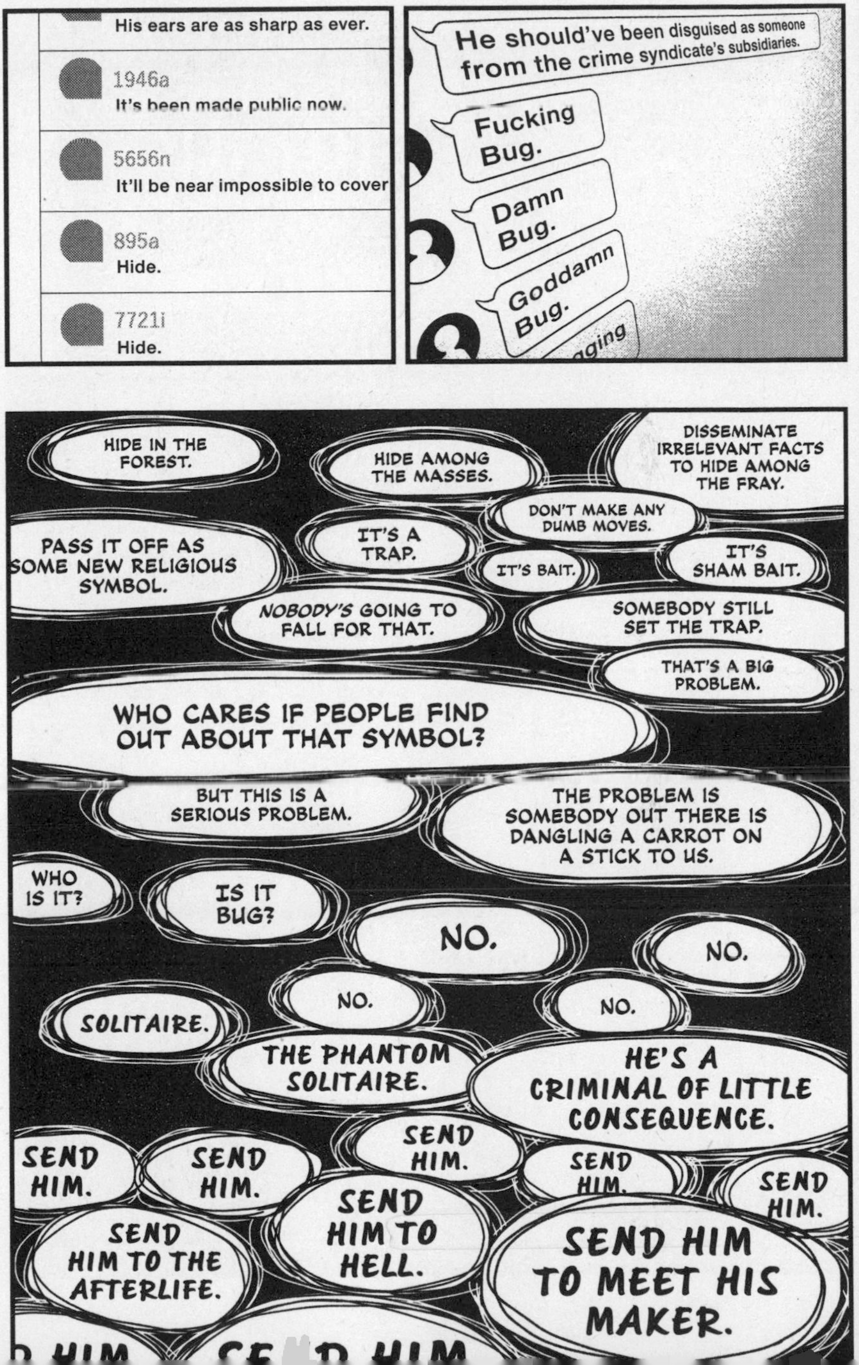
His ears are as sharp as ever.
1946a
It's been made public now.
5656n
It'll be near impossible to cover
895a
Hide.
7721i
Hide.
He should've been disguised as someone from the crime syndicate's subsidiaries.
Fucking Bug.
Damn Bug.
Goddamn Bug.
HIDE IN THE FOREST.
HIDE AMONG THE MASSES.
DISSEMINATE IRRELEVANT FACTS TO HIDE AMONG THE FRAY.
DON'T MAKE ANY DUMB MOVES.
PASS IT OFF AS SOME NEW RELIGIOUS SYMBOL.
IT'S A TRAP.
IT'S BAIT.
IT'S SHAM BAIT.
NOBODY'S GOING TO FALL FOR THAT.
SOMEBODY STILL SET THE TRAP.
THAT'S A BIG PROBLEM.
WHO CARES IF PEOPLE FIND OUT ABOUT THAT SYMBOL?
BUT THIS IS A SERIOUS PROBLEM.
THE PROBLEM IS SOMEBODY OUT THERE IS DANGLING A CARROT ON A STICK TO US.
WHO IS IT?
IS IT BUG?
NO.
NO.
NO.
NO.
SOLITAIRE.
THE PHANTOM SOLITAIRE.
HE'S A CRIMINAL OF LITTLE CONSEQUENCE.
SEND HIM.
SEND HIM.
SEND HIM.
SEND HIM.
SEND HIM.
SEND HIM TO THE AFTERLIFE.
SEND HIM TO HELL.
SEND HIM TO MEET HIS MAKER.

Make it quick.

And painless.

Don't even give him time to suffer.

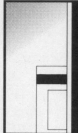

Sadism is refreshing, but if we indulge, we'll give away more information than we really should.

—Just like what happened five years ago.

WHAT THE HELL IS THIS...?

...IS THAT THE SYMBOL YOU WERE TALKING ABOUT?

...I GUESS THERE'S NO POINT HIDING IT NOW.

IT'S *NOT QUITE THE SAME.*

AND YOU SAY POLKA SHINO-YAMA DREW THIS?

to choose. He trusts nobody. On the west side of the place indicated, there's one more garage. There's a signpost. 383 mirror is eating into it.

IF SOLITAIRE'S RESPONSIBLE, THEN HE MUST ALSO HAVE SOME CONNECTION TO HOSOROGI-SAN......

YEAH.

EITHER WAY, IT MEANS WE'VE SEEN THIS SAME SYMBOL MULTIPLE TIMES NOW.

COULD HE BE PART OF THE GROUP HOSOROGI-SAN WAS FOLLOWING...?

OR... WAIT.

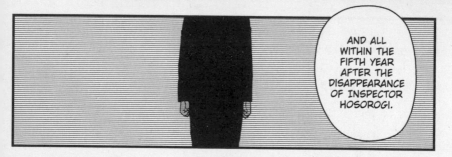

AND ALL WITHIN THE FIFTH YEAR AFTER THE DISAPPEARANCE OF INSPECTOR HOSOROGI.

IT'S POSSIBLE I'VE CAUGHT SOLITAIRE'S ATTENTION.

...YEAH.

RATHER THAN WRITE IT OFF AS A COINCIDENCE, DON'T YOU THINK WE SHOULD REGARD THEM AS CONNECTED IN SOME WAY?

OH, THERE YOU ARE! FOUND YOU! TSUBAKI-CHAN! TSUBAKI-CHAN!

HE MIGHT HAVE BEEN SPYING IN ON POLKA SHINOYAMA'S FORTUNE-TELLING SESSION REMOTELY.

IT'S STILL TOO SOON TO RULE ANYTHING OUT. WE NEED MORE INFORMA—

ME?

SUM-MONED... BY WHOM?

I KNOW NOW'S NOT A GOOD TIME, BUT YOU'RE BEING SUMMONED.

YAMADA-SAN?

METRO-POLITAN POLICE DEPART-MENT SAKURA-DAMON.

THE CENTRAL OFFICE.

AT THIS POINT, THERE'S PROBABLY MORE CHATTER ABOUT THIS ONLINE THAN ON THE OFFICIAL NEWS CHANNELS.

HM.

Both the city of Tokyo and the Metropolitan Police Department state that dirigibles are not permitted to fly in the airspace above the city.

PARARARA (FLIP)

AH!

DANG. EVEN FLYING SO LOW...

I PURCHASED AN ENTIRE FLEET OF DIRIGIBLES FROM THE GROCER.

ビュオオオ

BYUOOO (WHOOOO)

I REALLY TREATED MYSELF THIS TIME.

...THERE'S STILL QUITE A STRONG BREEZE UP HERE.

12

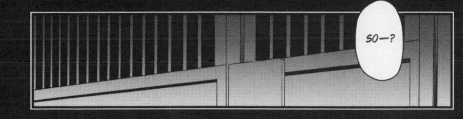

SO—?

THREE TRILLION YEN.

WHAT'S YOUR ASKING PRICE FOR THE INFORMATION?

ニコ

NIKO (SMILE)

PARDON?

・・・・・・

NO, NO, NO.

THREE TRILLION YEN.

THE ACTUAL AMOUNT HAD A NUMBER DOWN TO THE LAST DIGIT, BUT LET'S ROUND IT UP AND MAKE IT PRETTY.

HIJACKING THE RADIO WAVES FOR THREE MINUTES ALREADY COST ME THIRTY MILLION YEN, OKAY!?

NO, NO, NO. ARE YOU CRAZY!?

...AS I'VE ALREADY SAID...

...IN MY STORE, PRICES ARE DETERMINED BY THE PATRON'S FINANCIAL STANDING.

I DON'T GET IT. HOW'D YOU COME TO THREE TRILLION YEN?

AND "FINANCIAL STANDING"... REFERS TO THEIR WHOLE LIVES.

IF YOU WERE TO EMPLOY *EVERY POSSIBLE MEANS* AVAILABLE TO YOU AND POUR ALL YOUR EFFORTS INTO EARNESTLY EARNING MONEY...

...I CALCULATED THAT OVER THE COURSE OF A LIFETIME, YOU WOULD BE ABLE TO EARN SIX TRILLION YEN.

AND DO NOT MISUNDER-STAND.

THIS IS YOU WE'RE TALKING ABOUT.

IT'S BASIC MATH—THAT SYMBOL IS WORTH HALF YOUR LIFE.

HAD IT BEEN ANYONE ELSE WHO'D COME TO SEE ME...

...I WOULD'VE PROBABLY SOLD THE INFORMATION FOR A FEW TEN-YEN COINS.

ZUI (FWP)

BECAUSE, TO ANYBODY ELSE, THE TRUE MEANING OF THIS SYMBOL WOULD BE MERE NONSENSE.

MONEY BOX

BUT YOU'RE DIFFERENT.

MONEY BOX

IT WOULD BE ONLY AS VALUABLE AS CASUALLY CHEWING A GUMBALL.

GUMBALL

...THAT THE INFORMATION ABOUT THIS SYMBOL WILL CHANGE YOUR DESTINY. I WOULD EVEN GO SO FAR AS TO SAY THAT IT WOULD SERVE AS A MIRACLE DRUG SPECIFICALLY DESIGNED FOR YOU, THE PHANTOM SOLITAIRE.

I GUARANTEE...

NOW DON'T YOU AGREE THAT WHAT I'M ASKING FOR IS HARDLY UNREASONABLE?

LIKENED TO THE COST OF A PRESCRIPTION, IT'D COST YOU HALF OF ALL THE MONEY YOU'D EARN IN A LIFETIME...

USED THE WRONG WAY, IT COULD ALSO BECOME A HARMFUL TOXIN THAT COULD DESTROY YOU INSTEAD.

I TRUSTED YOUR PREDECESSOR, SO I ACCEPT WHAT YOU SAY.

...I SEE.

AFTER ALL YOU'VE SAID, IT'D BE NO FUN GETTING THE ANSWER NOW.

I'LL ARRIVE AT IT BY MY OWN METHODS.

I THINK THAT'D BE A WISE DECISION.

BUT I'M PUTTING THE DEAL ON HOLD.

I MEAN, I'LL STILL PAY YOU FOR ANY HELP I NEED.

I WANT TO FLY A NUMBER OF DIRIGIBLES OVER THE CITY VERY SOON. NEXT WEEK. HOW MUCH WILL THAT COST ME?

......

BESIDES, IT SHOULD BE FUN UNCOVERING THE MYSTERY STEP-BY-STEP.

......SINCE YOU'RE ONE OF MY BEST CUSTOMERS, I'LL GIVE YOU THIS WORD OF ADVICE, ON THE HOUSE.

WELL, WELL... THAT LOOK ON YOUR FACE TELLS ME...YOU'VE GUESSED WHAT I'VE GOT UP MY SLEEVE, EH?

POSU
(PLOP)
ぽすっ

YOU'VE INHERITED THAT DUTIFUL TENDENCY FROM YOUR PREDECES-SOR.

...PLEASE TAKE CARE OF YOURSELF.

EVEN I AM INCAPABLE OF RECOVERING A LOST LIFE.

THIS KNOWLEDGE BECOMING A HARMFUL TOXIN TO YOU WAS NOT SIMPLY A FIGURE OF SPEECH.

WHAT TRICKERY DID YOU USE TO EVADE THE OFFICERS' ATTENTION FOR SO LONG?

GII (CREAK)
ギィ

0000

YOU SAID IT'D ONLY TAKE FIVE MINUTES, BUT IT'S BEEN CLOSE TO TEN NOW.

WHY, IT'S REALLY VERY SIMPLE.

OH, COME, NOW. SHE'S THE NICE ONE.

THAT WAS VERY CRUEL OF YOU.

GATHER OUR MEN!

I OPENED THE DOOR TO THE YOUNGER OF THE GATOR SISTERS'S ROOM.

THOUGH, WELL...SHE'LL PROBABLY BE RESPONSIBLE FOR A LOT OF PROPERTY DAMAGE.

SHE WON'T KILL ANY COPS.

THE REPAIR COSTS WILL BE COVERED THANKS TO A "GENEROUS DONATION FROM A MYSTERIOUS FIGURE."

AND I'M SURE IT'LL BE MUCH CHEAPER THAN THREE TRILLION YEN.

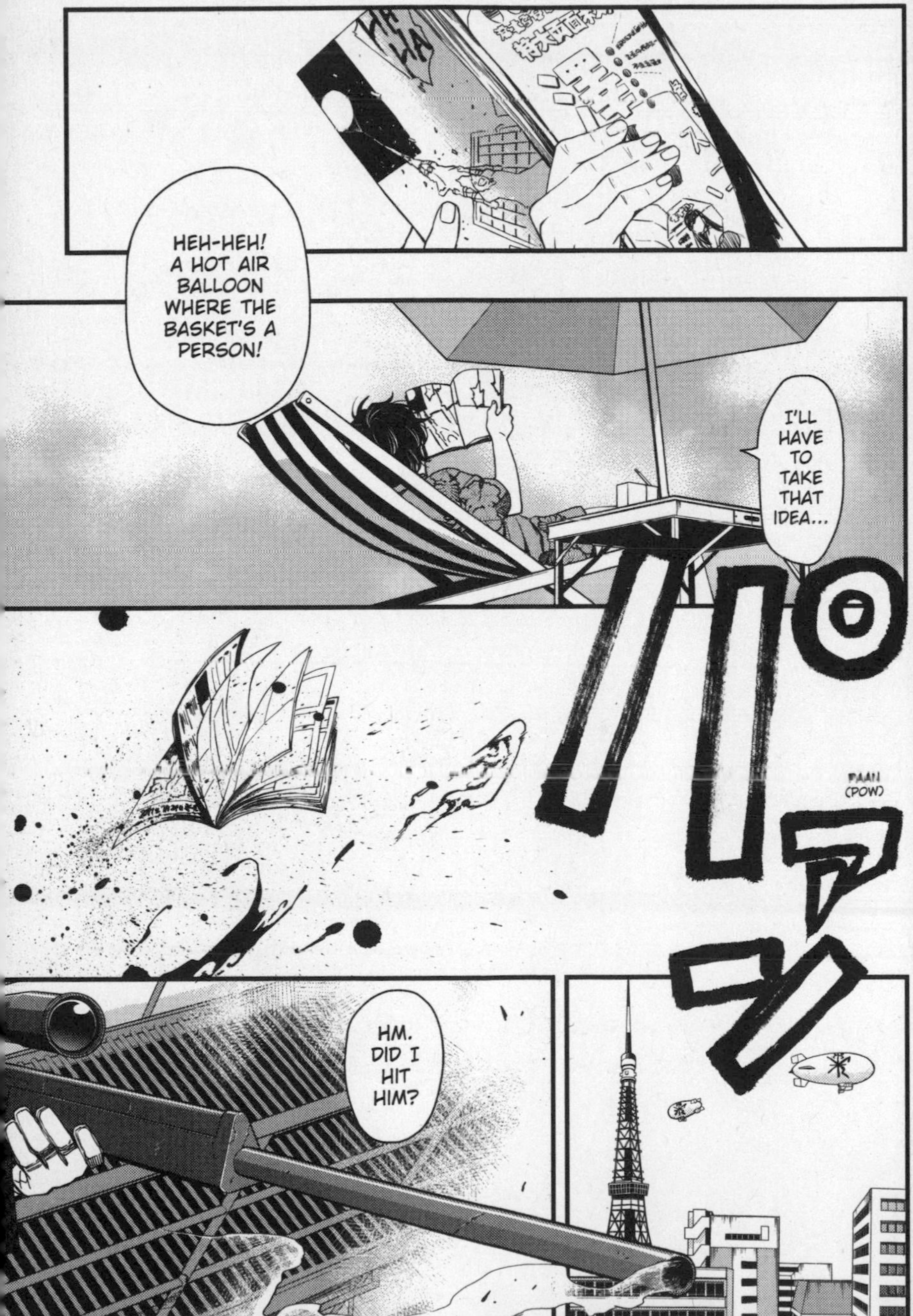
HEH-HEH! A HOT AIR BALLOON WHERE THE BASKET'S A PERSON!
I'LL HAVE TO TAKE THAT IDEA...
パァン
PAAN (POW)
HM. DID I HIT HIM?

SEE FOR YOURSELF.

?

IT SAYS, "YOU MISSED."

YOU MISSED.

HNGH. BETWEEN SHIBUYA AND IKEBUKURO, WE'RE NOT GETTING ANY GOOD JOBS.

IT'S PISSING ME OFF.

WHO KNOWS? BUT I DOUBT WE'LL GET PAID.

..DOES THAT MEAN THE MISSION'S FAILED?

YOU MISSED.

SHOULD WE GO TO SHINJUKU?

I'VE HEARD GOOD THINGS ABOUT THE MEDIATOR THERE.

The horror! A mysterious organization lurking in society!

...my dummy was shot by a sniper.

Fifty-eight minutes after the dirigibles went up...

II ▶I 🔊 ● LIVE

...is a police helicopter.

horror! ...ious ...ganization ...urking in society!

How could they have known I'd be up on top of the airship?

The only thing that could get high enough to see my position...

......And so, I have a proposal to you viewers watching at home.

In other words...an organization capable of arranging a hit on me in less than an hour has extended its reach into the police force.

And they could probably be called a secret organization. Don't you feel a titillating conspiracy at work here?

There are people out there who tried to silence me the moment this symbol was made public.

I'm sure you viewers out there are more than curious about what this symbol means. I am too.

Something that dangerous is at work in our world.

I'll pick whoever can give me the most helpful information on said organization and gift a few lucky souls three hundred million yen for their efforts!

I want to know about the organization affiliated with this symbol. Any relevant names or locations— I'll take anything.

24

I forgot to think up a good sign-off catchphr—

Ah!

Come after me to find out how to contact me! So until we meet again—!

If you're wondering if I'll really pay up, then look no further than my past works, okay?

BU
(CLICK)

...THAT'S A GOOD QUESTION.

チラッ
CHIRA
(GLANCE)

LET'S THINK ABOUT THIS LOGICALLY. WHERE DO WE START?

THAT'S... UM.

YEAH. WHAT DO WE DO, POLKA?

...THIS IS GETTING OUT OF HAND.

YEAH.

I WANT ANSWERS TOO.

THE NATIONAL EMBLEM OF A FALLEN EMPIRE.

...FROM THE WORLD I CAME FROM...

WHAT'S THIS ABOUT EMPIRES AND PAST LIVES...? WHAT'S GOING ON?

YOU'LL CERTAINLY TELL ME, WON'T YOU, POLKA?

...SURE.

ACHOO!!
FWOOT!!
AIR PURIFIER
TOTAL PROTECTION FACE MASK
ONE SIZE FITS MOST
NASAL INFLAMMATION + DUST ALLERGY
THAT'S THE ONLY PLACE WITH SUPER-CLEAN AIR.

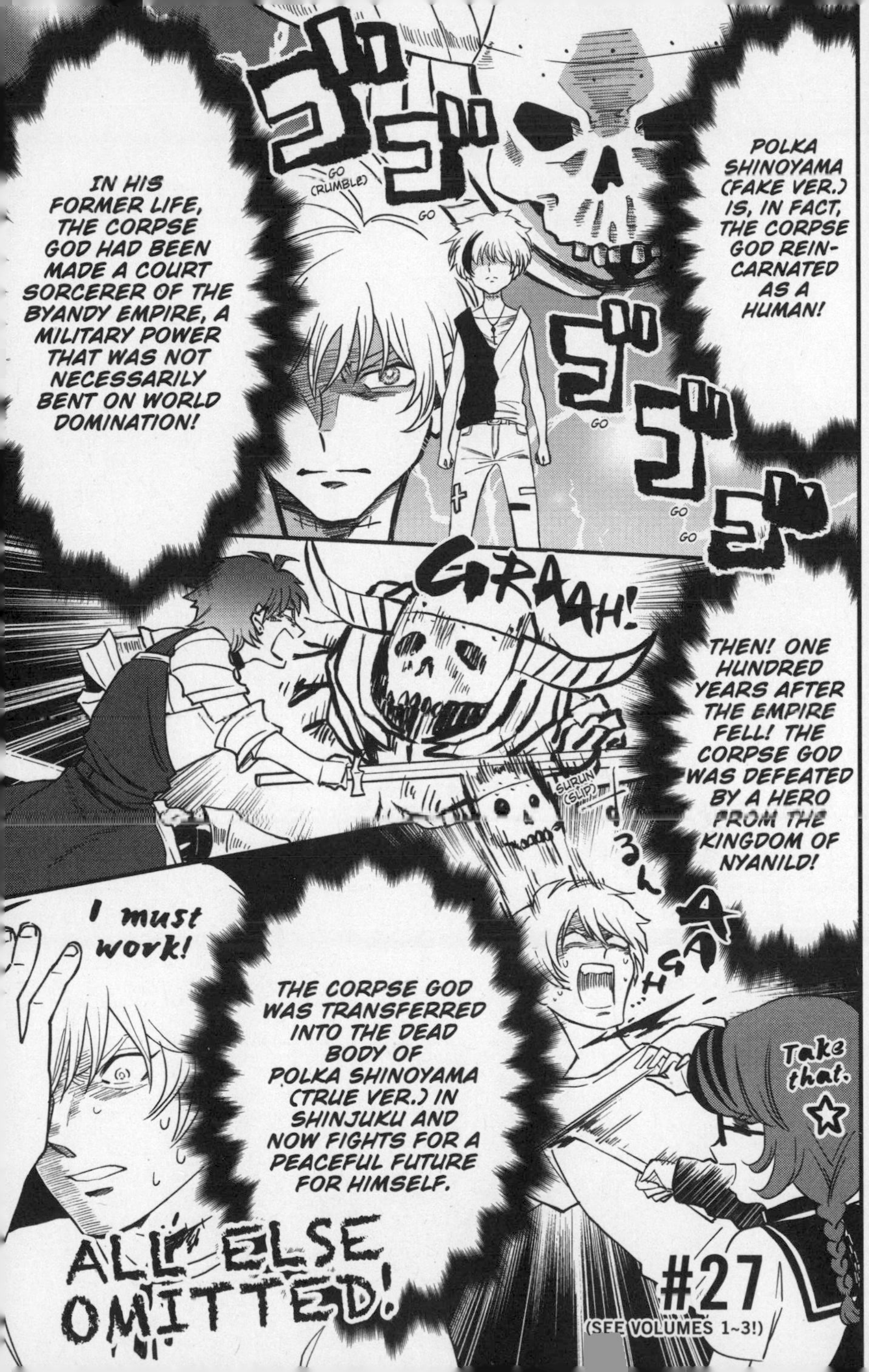

POLKA SHINOYAMA (FAKE VER.) IS, IN FACT, THE CORPSE GOD REIN-CARNATED AS A HUMAN!
GO (RUMBLE)
GO
IN HIS FORMER LIFE, THE CORPSE GOD HAD BEEN MADE A COURT SORCERER OF THE BYANDY EMPIRE, A MILITARY POWER THAT WAS NOT NECESSARILY BENT ON WORLD DOMINATION!
GO
GO
GO
THEN! ONE HUNDRED YEARS AFTER THE EMPIRE FELL! THE CORPSE GOD WAS DEFEATED BY A HERO FROM THE KINGDOM OF NYANILD!
GRAAAH!
SURUN (SLIP)
HGAA
I must work!
THE CORPSE GOD WAS TRANSFERRED INTO THE DEAD BODY OF POLKA SHINOYAMA (TRUE VER.) IN SHINJUKU AND NOW FIGHTS FOR A PEACEFUL FUTURE FOR HIMSELF.
Take that. ☆
ALL ELSE OMITTED!
#27
(SEE VOLUMES 1~3!)

#27

......AND THERE YOU HAVE IT.

THE SOUL OF THE TRUE POLKA-KUN IS SAFE, AND I WILL RETURN HIM TO HIS BODY IN DUE TIME.

......

I SEE HE DOESN'T WANT TO TELL ME THE TRUTH... FINE. I GIVE UP. HRMPH, HUMPH, HUMPH!

I THINK IT'LL ACTUALLY BE EASIER IF SHE DOESN'T BELIEVE IT......

HISO

HISO (PSST)

HOW CAN YOU EXPECT HER TO BELIEVE THAT STORY!?

HISO

I BELIEVE YOU.

I SEE...

WOW.

YOU DO!?

THE WAY YOU REMAINED SO CALM WHEN THAT OFFICER GRABBED YOU BY THE SHIRT DURING YOUR FORTUNE-TELLING SESSION WAS NOTHING LIKE THE POLKA I KNOW.

I COULD ALREADY TELL YOU WEREN'T POLKA.

BUT I'M STILL CONFUSED.

AHH...

......

MONI
(MOOSH)
もに
もに

MUGYUU
(SQUEEZE)
むぎゅう

PART OF ME
DOESN'T WANT
TO BELIEVE
THAT ANYONE
WOULD KILL
POLKA, BUT...

......

HUH?
WHAT?

MONI
MONI
もに
もに

BEFORE I
ASK FOR
MORE
DETAILS, I'M
GOING TO
GO TAKE A
SHOWER AND
CLEAR MY
HEAD.

UHH......
SHE'S
HARD TO
GET A
READING
ON...

PATAN
(SHUT)
パタン

AND I WON'T
SAY ANYTHING
TO XIAOYU
WHEN HE GETS
BACK FROM
HIS SHOPPING
TRIP, SO DON'T
WORRY.

OH...

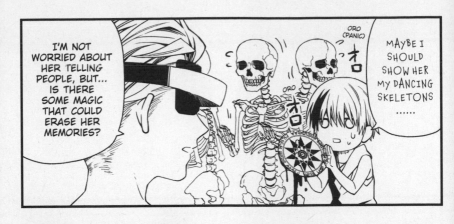

I'M NOT WORRIED ABOUT HER TELLING PEOPLE, BUT... IS THERE SOME MAGIC THAT COULD ERASE HER MEMORIES?

ORO

ORO (PANIC)

オロ

MAYBE I SHOULD SHOW HER MY DANCING SKELETONS ......

SO YOU BASICALLY MAKE THE SOUL INTO A SCALPEL TO CUT OUT A PIECE OF YOUR VICTIM'S SOUL.

THAT AFFECTS THE BRAIN ITSELF.

MEMORY

SPIRIT

THERE'S A NECROMANTIC METHOD WHERE I USE A SOUL TO POSSESS THE SPIRIT OF MY VICTIM AND CUT OUT A PIECE OF HER MEMORY.

HONESTLY, IT'S NOT THAT BAD, BUT...I'VE ONLY KNOWN IT TO BE USED ON PEOPLE FROM THE WORLD I COME FROM.

IS IT A TRICKY SPELL TO PULL OFF?

IT'S A DIFFERENT SYSTEM OF MAGIC FROM THAT USED BY THE MEMBERS OF GELDWOOD, WHO BRAINWASH AND USE CONFESSIONAL SPELLS...

...THEN, TO SOME DEGREE, DOING IT SLOPPILY AND BREAKING THEIR MINDS WOULD BE BETTER.

BUT IF THE VICTIM IS CLEARLY AN ENEMY...

......

AAAH... THEN WE CAN'T JUST TEST IT OUT WILLY-NILLY...

IF THERE'S SOME FATAL DIFFERENCE BETWEEN THEM AND THE PEOPLE OF THIS WORLD, ONE SMALL MISTAKE COULD LEAVE HER DISABLED.

HUUUH ...?

THEY'VE PROBABLY LOST CONSCIOUSNESS, SO THEY WON'T BE TESTIFYING AGAINST US.

CARELESS ATTITUDE

BU!!

YES, BUT TO A LESSER EXTENT.

SO THAT THEY WOULDN'T BECOME COMPLETELY DISABLED.

DON'T TELL ME...YOU DID THIS MEMORY MANIPULATION THING... ON THOSE THUGS?

I KNEW IT...... SOMETIMES, YOU SCARE ME.

WHAT?

HAAAAH...

...MAKES ME A BIT HAPPY.

...HEARING YOU SAY IT'S ONLY "SOME-TIMES"...

...EXCITING.

IT WAS SOOO...

THOUGH, SHE WAS ACTUALLY HAPPY ABOUT IT...

WELL, EVEN THOUGH YOU SCARE ME, IT'S NOTHING COMPARED TO HOW MISAKI MUST FEEL, CONSIDERING YOU KILLED HER AND ALL.

?

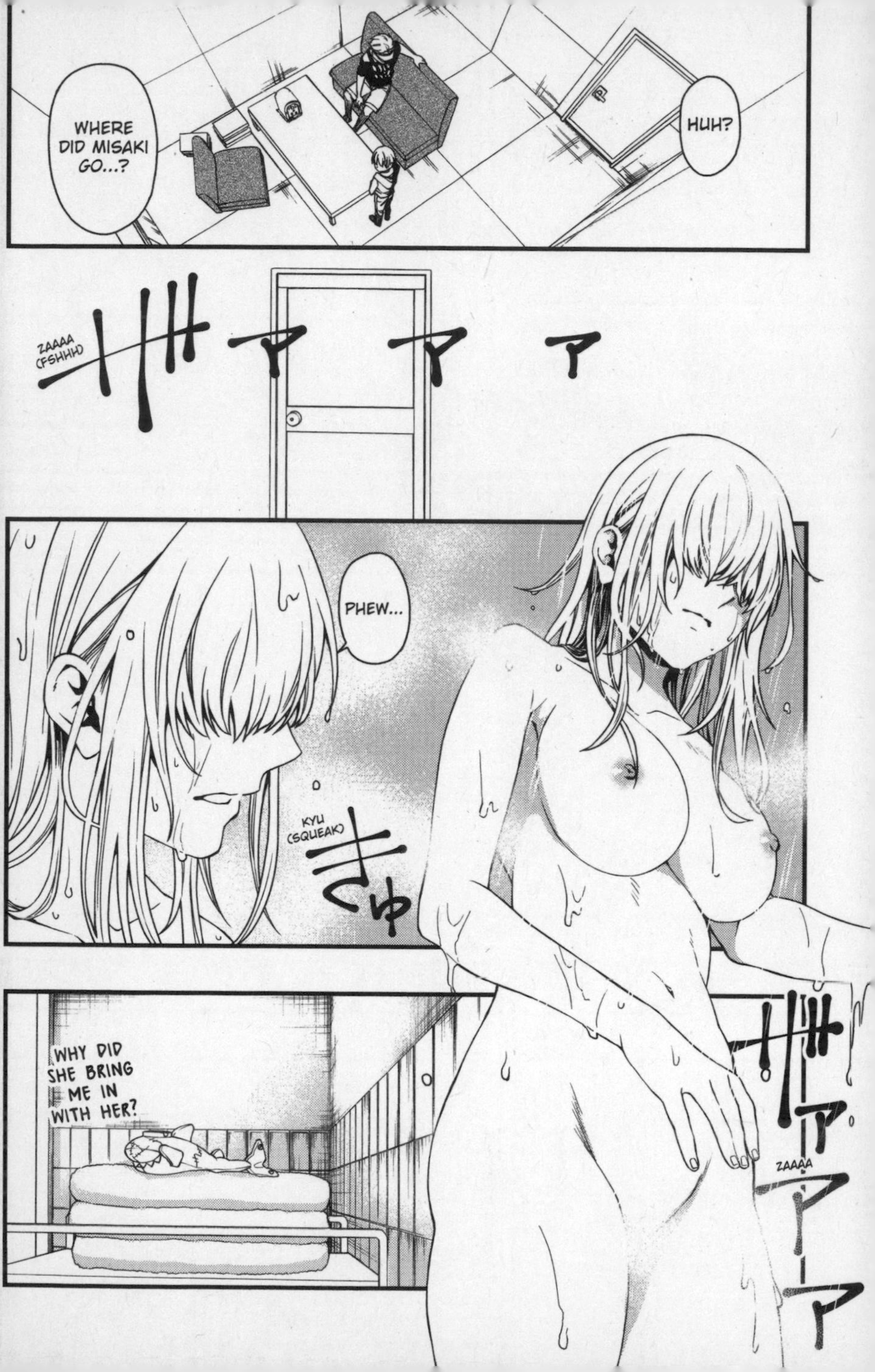
HUH?
WHERE DID MISAKI GO...?
ザァァァ
ZAAAA (FSHHH)
PHEW...
きゅ
KYU (SQUEAK)
ザァァーァ
ZAAAA
WHY DID SHE BRING ME IN WITH HER?

BUT I'M JUST GETTING OUT.

I CAME TO TAKE A SHOWER TOO!

...OH.

—!?

BIKU (JUMP)

KEE HEE HEE!

I SWEAR IT!

I'M NOT LOOKING!

I SEE NO-FIN!

THEN WHY DON'T WE TALK WHILE WE GET CHANGED?

OH!

GABA (YANK)

AFTER HEARING THAT...

...AREN'T YOU CURIOUS...

YEAH!

TALK?

...WHO IT WAS THAT KILLED POLKA-KUN?

こつ

KO
(BONK)

OR...

...DO YOU ALREADY KNOW AND DON'T CARE?

KEE HEE HEE!

I DON'T LIKE WHEN PEOPLE DODGE MY QUESTIONS.

...I'D RATHER WE TALK ABOUT SHARKS.

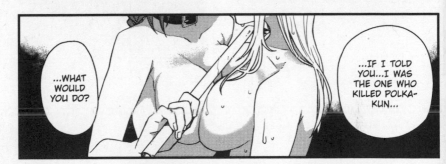

...WHAT WOULD YOU DO?

...IF I TOLD YOU...I WAS THE ONE WHO KILLED POLKA-KUN...

SO... THAT'S HOW IT IS.

...AH. I SEE.

PICHON (PLIP)

......!

YOU...WANT SOMEONE TO *REVILE* YOU, DON'T YOU?

WHEN HE SEES THE MAN-EATING SHARK FINALLY GET KILLED IN A MOVIE, HE'LL SAY, "I FEEL BAD FOR ALL THE PEOPLE WHO GOT EATEN BUT ALSO FOR THE SHARK."

HE'S A NICE KID LIKE THAT.

POLKA'S *FORGIVEN* YOU, HASN'T HE?

BUT I BET POLKA FORGAVE YOU FOR KILLING HIM.

I INTEND TO ASK HIM MORE ABOUT WHAT EXACTLY WENT DOWN.

......

SO YOU THOUGHT YOU'D GET ME TO HATE ON YOU SO YOU COULD FEEL A LITTLE ATONEMENT FOR WHAT YOU'VE DONE.

...YOU STILL HAVEN'T COME TO TERMS WITH IT, HAVE YOU?

BUT IT'S OKAY.

I FORGIVE YOU.

KO (BONK)

SLY GIRL.

AND I WON'T REVILE YOU.

FOR ME, SHARK FILMS ARE TEXTBOOKS, SCHOOL, LOVERS, AND FAMILY.

...?

KEE-HEE-HEE...YOU'RE SHARP. YOU REMIND ME OF A DETECTIVE.

AFTER WATCHING AS MANY SHARK FILMS AS I HAVE, YOU GET A KNACK FOR THESE THINGS.

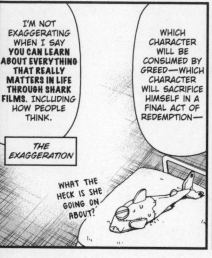

I'M NOT EXAGGERATING WHEN I SAY YOU CAN LEARN ABOUT EVERYTHING THAT REALLY MATTERS IN LIFE THROUGH SHARK FILMS. INCLUDING HOW PEOPLE THINK.

WHICH CHARACTER WILL BE CONSUMED BY GREED—WHICH CHARACTER WILL SACRIFICE HIMSELF IN A FINAL ACT OF REDEMPTION—

THE EXAGGERATION

WHAT THE HECK IS SHE GOING ON ABOUT?

I'M NOT SCARED, NO.

...SO YOU'RE NOT SCARED OF ME?

EVEN THOUGH...I'M AN ASSASSIN WHO SLIT POLKA-KUN'S THROAT?

WHY NOT?

BECAUSE ANYBODY WHO LIKES SHARK FILMS CAN'T BE A BAD PERSON.

...UM, OKAAAAY.

I LOVE HOW, BEFORE MATING WITH A FEMALE, THE MALE WILL FAST!

NICE...

LAST NIGHT

...WHAT DO YOU THINK ABOUT SHARK MATING HABITS?

I'VE ONLY KNOWN YOU FOR A LITTLE WHILE, BUT I'VE ENJOYED TALKING ABOUT SHARKS AND SHARK FILMS WITH YOU.

...???

THERE'S NO WAY SOMEONE WHO CAN TALK ABOUT SHARKS AND SHARK FILMS COULD EVER BE A BAD GUY.

EVEN IF YOU SLIT MY OWN FLESH AND BLOOD'S THROAT, SHARKS FORGIVE YOU.

I HEAR NO-FIN!

...DECIDED TO HAVE NEVER HEARD ANY OF IT IN THE FIRST PLACE.

HAVING TO WITNESS THAT CHILLING REALITY, THE SOUL OF POLKA SHINOYAMA...

NONE OF THIS MAKES ANY SENSE...

THE SCREWS WERE EVEN LOOSER IN HIS RELATIVE'S HEAD THAN POLKA HAD IMAGINED.

44

...AND THERE'S ALSO THE FACT THAT YOU SAVED MY LITTLE BROTHER AND SISTER, SHIZUKI AND KAZUKI.

IT'S NOT MUCH, BUT THAT'S MY SECOND REASON.

...

...KEE HEE...!

I SEE......... SO THAT'S THE LESSER, "SECONDARY" REASON...!

AH-HA-HA-HA-HA!

THAT DOES IT.

OKAY.

IN THAT CASE...

I DON'T EVEN KNOW...

...WHAT TO SAY AT THIS POINT.

KEE HEE HEE!

...WHY DON'T WE TALK ABOUT SHARKS?

SFX: MOCCHIRI (PRESS), SUBE (SMOOTH) SUBE

BUT MY TEST FAILED!

AND SO, I THOUGHT I'D TEST SAYO-CHAN TO SEE IF SHE WAS THE ONE WHO PUT THAT HIT ON YOU, SEE?

46

UH-HUH. OKAY.

KEE HEE HEE!

STILL, I DON'T THINK SAYO-CHAN HAD ANYTHING TO DO WITH YOUR MURDER, POLKA-KUN.

HOW RUDE. IT'S SIMPLY THAT MY BRAIN'S NOT INTERESTED IN ANYTHING THAT ISN'T TO DO WITH SHARKS.

ALL WE'VE LEARNED FROM WHAT YOU TOLD US IS THAT SHE'S CRAZY...?

THAT'S WHY I'D NEVER PUT A HIT ON POLKA.

I DON'T SEE HOW THOSE TWO THINGS ARE CONNECTED...

ARE YOU AN IDIOT?

...WHAT DO YOU THINK YOU'RE DOING?

WHY DOES THAT MAKE SENSE...

AND IF I WERE GOING TO KILL HIM, OBVIOUSLY, *I'D FEED HIM TO THE SHARKS.*

HM? WHAT DOES IT MATTER...?

DON'T TELL ME YOU TOOK THIS PLUSHIE INTO THE SHOWER WITH YOU.

BATH SHARK

...HM?

I FEEL BAD THIS IS THE KIND OF FAMILY YOU HAVE TO DEAL WITH, BUD...

SHARK CYBORG PLUSHIE...

SORRY FOR BORROWING THAT SHARK CYBORG PLUSHIE WITHOUT ASKING YOU.

DID YOU BRING HIM IN WITH YOU BECAUSE *YOU DON'T KNOW?*

...WAIT A SECOND.

.......?

HOW...

H-H-H-HOW...

YOU MAY HAVE NOT REALIZED IT, BUT I STILL FEEL FOR YOU, HAVING HAD SOMEONE WATCH YOU GET UNDRESSED...

HOW CAN THIS BE...?

ずーーん

ZULULUN (GLOOM)

PESHI PESHI (SMACK)

ペシ ペシ

I SAAAW NOTHIIIING!

ROZAN-SAN SAID THE SAME THING...

YOU REALLY ARE FAMILY.

JI (STARE)

じ、

I THOUGHT FOR SURE THAT THERE WERE TWO SOULS COMPETING AGAINST EACH OTHER IN THAT ONE BODY...

I CAN'T BELIEVE A MEMBER OF MY OWN FAMILY'S BECOME A SHARK!

が"ば"っ

GABA (JUMP)

THAT'S NOT THE PROBLEM HERE!

IT'S NOT?

WHY!?

LISTEN... I'LL GIVE YOU MY BODY, POLKA.

SO PLEASE MAKE ME A SHARK!

I SAY NO-FIN!

I CAN'T EVEN FOLLOW THIS CONVER-SATION...

POLKA'S SOUL DECIDED NOT TO ASK ANY QUESTIONS.

THIS SYMBOL MEANS SOMETHING TO YOU, RIGHT?

ANYWAY, WE HAVE SOMETHING IMPORTANT TO DISCUSS HERE, POLKA.

POLKA-KUN WANTED TO BECOME A ROBOT.

MONI CMOOSHD

AH!

YOU CAN'T... SHE'S ALREADY LOST HER BRAIN TO SHARK FILMS.

50

...THEN I NEED TO FIND THEM.

IT'S JUST...... IF THERE ARE PEOPLE OUT THERE USING THIS SYMBOL TO DO SOMETHING...

IT'S NOT A PROBLEM THAT IT'S BEEN MADE PUBLIC.

...ASSUMING THIS SYMBOL REALLY DOES LINK BACK TO MY HOMELAND...

WHAT ABOUT LIVING A PEACEFUL LIFE?

IT'S A VERY SIGNIFICANT MEMORY FOR...US.

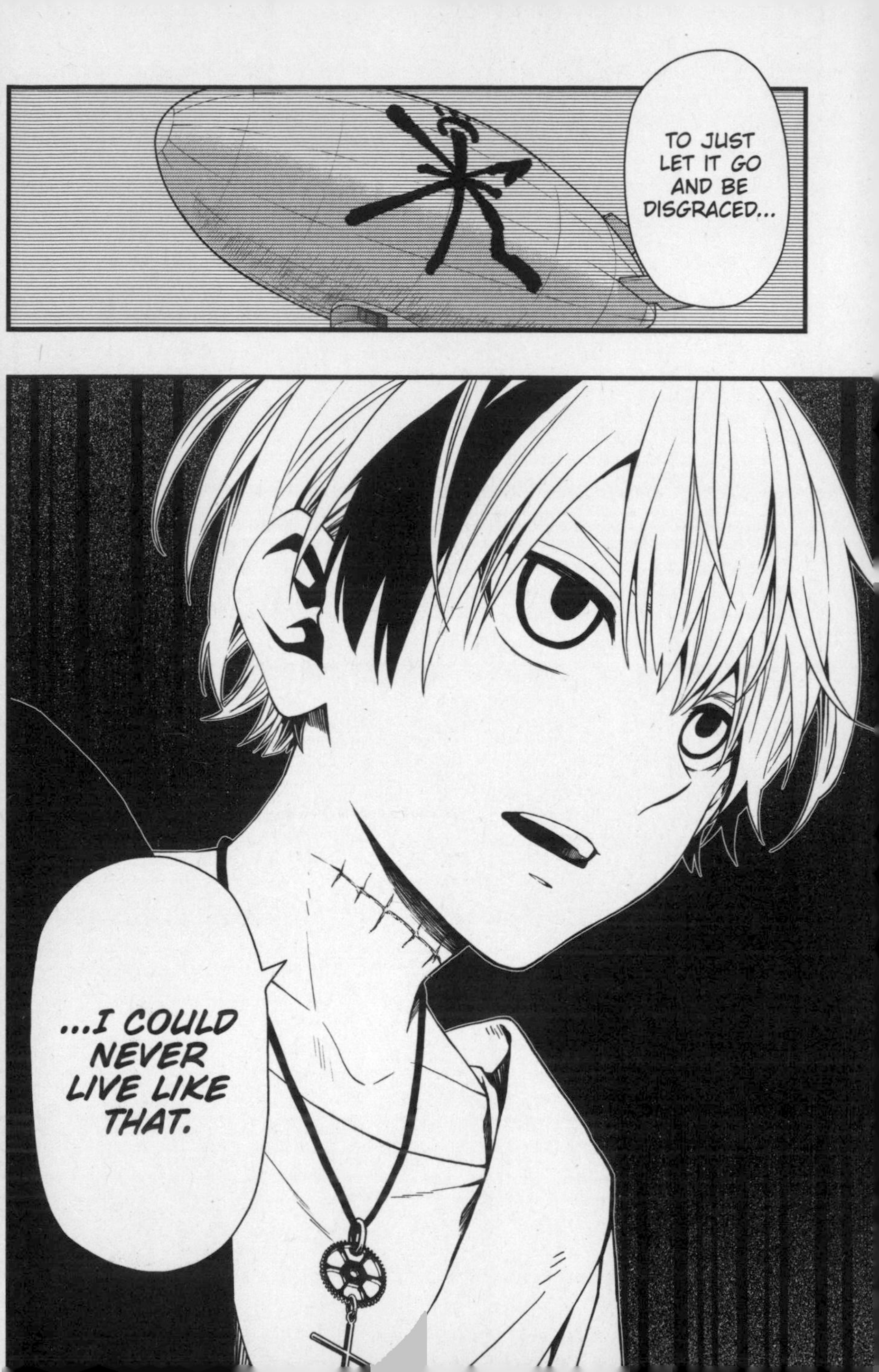
TO JUST LET IT GO AND BE DISGRACED...
...I COULD NEVER LIVE LIKE THAT.

I GET WHAT YOU WANT TO DO, POLKA.

BASICALLY, YOU WANT TO SEE IF THERE REALLY IS SOME SHADOW ORGANIZATION USING THAT SYMBOL OR NOT, RIGHT?

...THOUGH, IT'S ENTIRELY POSSIBLE THERE'S NO ORGANIZATION, AND SOLITAIRE IS JUST PULLING A STUNT.

#28

...IS A WIZARD FROM THE SAME WORLD POLKA-KUN CAME FROM?

THEN WOULDN'T THAT MEAN SOLITAIRE...

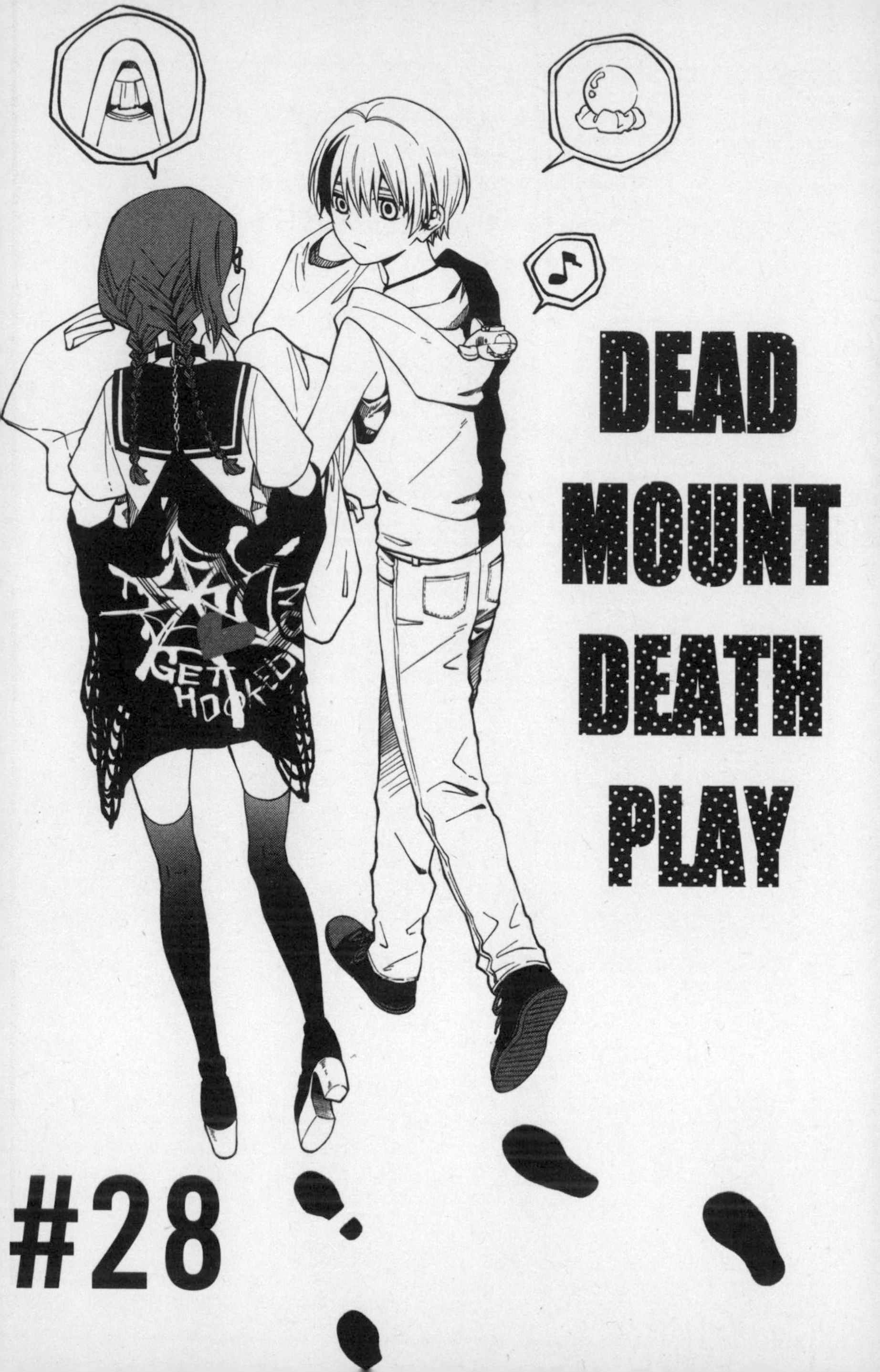
DEAD MOUNT DEATH PLAY
#28

BY THE WAY, POLKA, CAN YOU USE THOSE IDENTIFICATION SPELLS YOU ALWAYS SEE IN MANGA?

NO... HE WANTED INFORMATION ABOUT THAT SYMBOL.

...SO IT'S LIKELIER HE DOESN'T KNOW WHAT IT IS EITHER...

CAN'T YOU IDENTIFY WHO IT IS BY USING SOMETHING LIKE THAT?

TITLE:
LEGENDARY CHALLENGER

LV 99
HP 999 / 999
MP 999 / 999
ATTACK 999
DEFENSE 999
SPEED 999
DEXTERITY 999
CHARM 999

YOU KNOW HOW, LIKE, BY JUST LOOKING AT SOMEONE, YOU CAN SEE WHAT THEIR LEVEL, OCCUPATION, AND SKILLS ARE.

HUH?

...BUT ISN'T THAT LIKE WHAT YOU WERE DOING DURING MY FORTUNE-TELLING, TAKUMI-KUN?

OH YEAH. NOW THAT YOU MENTION IT, THERE'S MEMORIES ABOUT THAT IN THIS BODY...

LIB...RA?

STATS ACQUIRED!

NAME → NAME
OCCUPATION → WORK HISTORY
SKILLS → QUALIFICATIONS
STATS → MEDICAL RECORDS
PHYSICAL EXAM RESULTS
CRIMES → CRIMINAL RECORD
TRAFFIC VIOLATIONS, ETC.

USE THE CLIENT'S NAME TO CRACK THEIR DEFENSES!

POLKA SHINOYAMA

THAT'S ENOUGH JOKING AROUND, THANKS.

DOES NOT WORK ON HIGH-LEVEL PEOPLE (WHO HAVE HIGH SECURITY).

WAS I...... AN IDENTIFICATION WIZARD...?

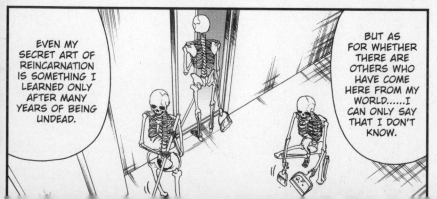

EVEN MY SECRET ART OF REINCARNATION IS SOMETHING I LEARNED ONLY AFTER MANY YEARS OF BEING UNDEAD.

BUT AS FOR WHETHER THERE ARE OTHERS WHO HAVE COME HERE FROM MY WORLD......I CAN ONLY SAY THAT I DON'T KNOW.

TO BE HONEST, EVEN AS A SUMMONER, I'M JUST AS SHOCKED THAT I WAS ABLE TO CALL THEM WITH SO LITTLE EFFORT.

HUH? BUT WEREN'T THESE BONE GUYS CALLED HERE FROM THE WORLD YOU LIVED IN, POLKA-KUN?

MORE ACCURATELY SPEAKING, THE "BONES" ARE MADE BY ATTRACTING ELEMENTS OF NEARBY STONE AND METAL, AND THEN MAKING THOSE TEMPORARY VESSELS FOR THE SOULS THAT I'VE SUMMONED.

IN A WORST-CASE SCENARIO, I'D SUMMON THEM IN THEIR ORIGINAL FORM, BUT THAT EATS UP A LOT OF MY MAGIC.

AN EXAMPLE OF A WORST-CASE SCENARIO

AREN'T THERE HUMAN SPIRITS THAT COULD TALK MORE?

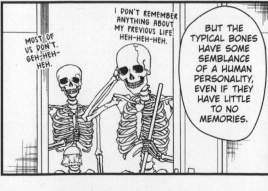

I DON'T REMEMBER ANYTHING ABOUT MY PREVIOUS LIFE! HEH-HEH-HEH.

MOST OF US DON'T. GEH-HEH-HEH.

BUT THE TYPICAL BONES HAVE SOME SEMBLANCE OF A HUMAN PERSONALITY, EVEN IF THEY HAVE LITTLE TO NO MEMORIES.

THOUGH THERE ARE STILL SOME WHO MAINTAIN THEIR CONTRACT WITH ME......

...MOST OF THEM WERE RELEASED DURING THE HUNDRED YEARS UP UNTIL THE LAST SUBJUGATION UNIT CAME.

BUT AFTER I MADE AN ENEMY OUT OF THE ORDER...

...THERE...

...ARE.

...I'M NOT SURE HOW I COULD POSSIBLY FACE THEM IF I WERE TO SUMMON THEM...

...ONCE I CAME TO BE SEEN AND TREATED AS A "WORLD DISASTER"...

NO MORE MOPING.

SO AT THE VERY LEAST, OUR MEMORIES—

WHENEVER YOU WANT TO SUMMON THEM, JUST DO IT WITH A SMILE.

IF THEY GET MAD AT YOU OR LASH OUT AT YOU, THEN JUST APOLOGIZE.

THEY CONTRACTED THEIR SOULS TO YOU BECAUSE THEY TRUST IN YOU. SO YOU TRUST IN THEM.

...IS THAT...

...REALLY ENOUGH FOR THEM TO FORGIVE ME...?

SAYO-SAN...

SO MUCH FOR THE POSSIBILITY THAT SAYO-SAN IS THE ACTUAL CRIMINAL BEHIND THE ATTEMPT ON THE REAL POLKA-KUN'S LIFE...

IF THAT WERE THE CASE, I GUESS SHE'D HAVE TAKEN CARE OF ME ALREADY.

じいいいん
(TOUCHED)

I'M SORRY FOR EVER DOUBTING YOU.

THAT'S WHAT WE NEED RIGHT NOW!

WHAT JUST HAPPENED? ARE SHARKS HIJACKING THE CONVERSATION?

ALSO...IF NECROMANCERS LIKE YOU EXIST, THEN THERE MUST ALSO BE SHARKMANCERS ...!

YOU DON'T HAVE TO ANSWER HONESTLY, YOU KNOW?

Deep-Sea Wizards
The Three Grimrope Sisters

THERE WERE PEOPLE WHO COULD MANIPULATE SCHOOLS OF FISH IN THE SEA, BUT......

I'M WAITING FOR INFORMATION.

WHAT DO WE DO?

BUT EVEN THAT SOLITAIRE MAN IS AFTER INFORMATION ON IT.

ANYWAY, THE ISSUE RIGHT NOW IS WHAT WE'RE GOING TO DO ABOUT THAT SYMBOL, RIGHT?

SOUNDS LIKE A JOB FOR ME.

NOW THEN... LIKE THAT SOLITAIRE GOON SAID HIMSELF, FIRST, I'LL SEE WHAT I CAN LEARN FROM THE COPS......

...

JUST LEAVE IT TO AN "IDENTIFICATION WIZARD" LIKE YOURS TRULY.

I'M THE RIGHT MAN IN THE RIGHT PLACE.

YOU'RE EXCITED ABOUT THIS.

REALLY!?

I can't go into detail about it yet, but that's not to say I don't have an inkling.

KA (CLAK)

KA

KA

KA

I can only speak about one department there, but the police department as a whole is more of a hotbed of vice than you think.

Except...... I know it's too late to stop you, but...

...whatever you do, be careful about it.

KA

KA

62

NOT AT ALL.

HEY, SORRY FOR CALLING YOU OUT HERE ALL OF A SUDDEN.

IT'LL BE A HUGE HELP HAVING YOU WITH ME, SENIOR COMMISSIONER HABAKI.

AND HERE, I'D BEEN HOPING YOUR CAREER PATH COULD BE STRAIGHT AND NARROW.

...DON'T LET HIM GET TO YOU.

TON (THUMP)
とん

THE SUPERINTENDENT GENERAL KNOWS HOW TO USE HIS FACE TO HIS ADVANTAGE.

...

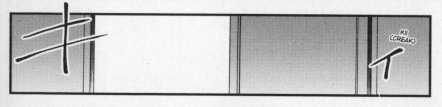

KON (KNOCK)
KON

KII (CREAK)

"TSUBAKI IWANOME-KUN," WAS IT?

SO YOU'RE THE ONE IN CHARGE OF THE SOLITAIRE CASE...

YOU LOOK LESS LIKE A POLICE OFFICER AND MORE LIKE A HOST FROM A CLUB OR SOMETHING.

OH WELL. YOUR DUTY IS YOUR DUTY. I'LL JUST ASSUME YOUR PIERCINGS AND DYE JOB ARE FOR THE SAKE OF DISGUISING YOURSELF.

...YES, SIR.

AND THAT IS...

...WHETHER YOU CAN BE A GEAR THAT HELPS TO TURN THIS ORGANIZATION OR NOT.

ONLY ONE THING MATTERS.

KO...
(CLAK)

I HOPE OUR RE- SPECTIVE COGS...

...MESH WELL WITH EACH OTHER.

SUPERINTENDENT GENERAL

JIROTAROU TAKANOSU

YOU THINK SO...?

WHAT A HUNK!

I KNOW IT'S NOT GOOD TO JUDGE A PERSON BY THEIR FACE, BUT HE LOOKS SCARY...

SO THIS IS THE CURRENT SUPERIN- TENDENT GENERAL...

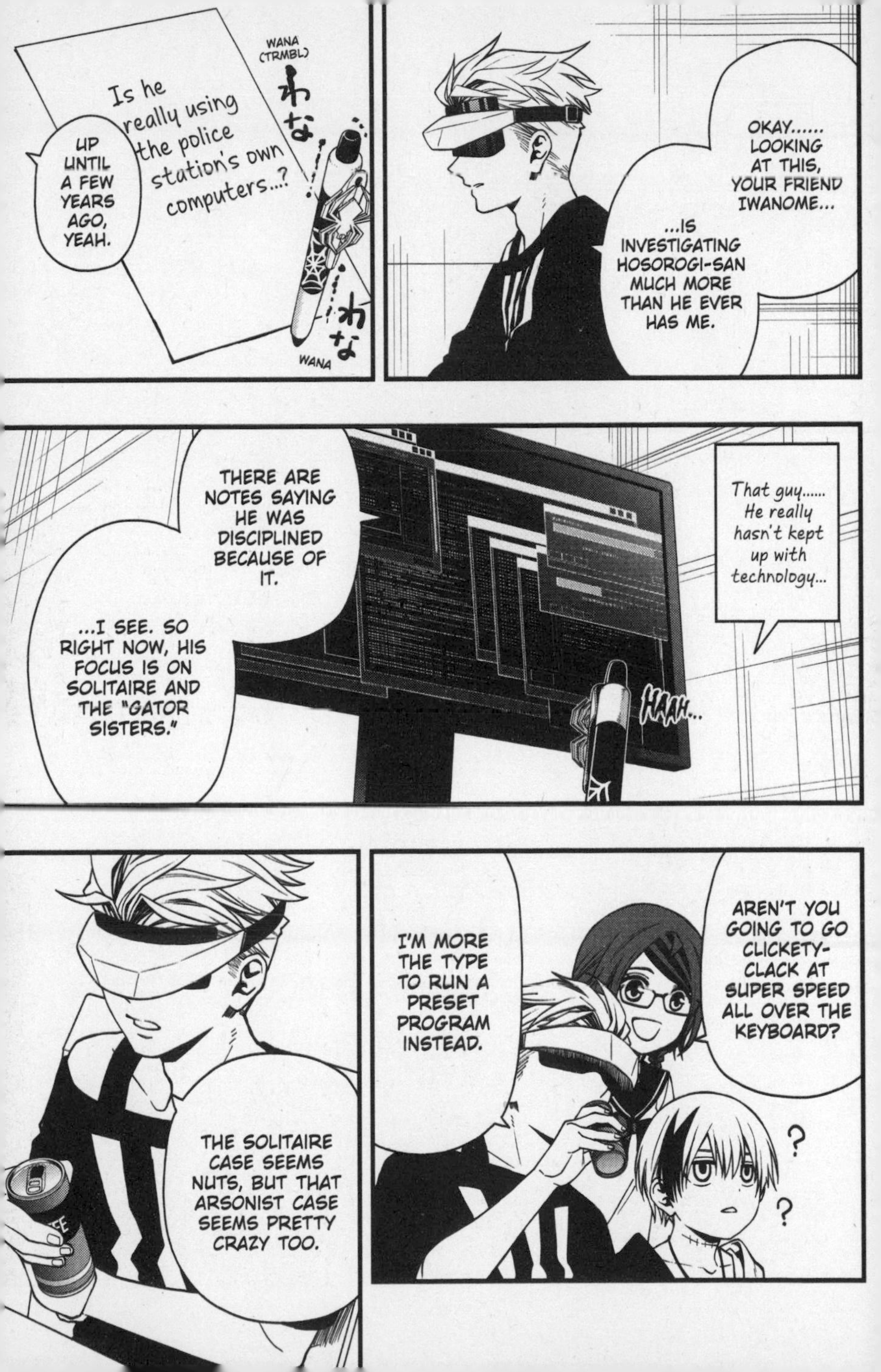
OKAY...... LOOKING AT THIS, YOUR FRIEND IWANOME...
...IS INVESTIGATING HOSOROGI-SAN MUCH MORE THAN HE EVER HAS ME.
WANA (TRMBL)
わな
Is he really using the police station's own computers...?
UP UNTIL A FEW YEARS AGO, YEAH.
わな
WANA
That guy...... He really hasn't kept up with technology...
HAAH...
THERE ARE NOTES SAYING HE WAS DISCIPLINED BECAUSE OF IT.
...I SEE. SO RIGHT NOW, HIS FOCUS IS ON SOLITAIRE AND THE "GATOR SISTERS."
AREN'T YOU GOING TO GO CLICKETY-CLACK AT SUPER SPEED ALL OVER THE KEYBOARD?
I'M MORE THE TYPE TO RUN A PRESET PROGRAM INSTEAD.
?
?
THE SOLITAIRE CASE SEEMS NUTS, BUT THAT ARSONIST CASE SEEMS PRETTY CRAZY TOO.

THE ONE THAT BURNED UP MY SHARKS...?

ARSON...? YOU MEAN THE ONE WHO STARTED THE FIRE AT THE SHINOYAMA ESTATE?

CALM DOWN— HE'S ALREADY DEAD.

IT LOOKS LIKE THE SHINOYAMA ARSONIST WAS COPYING FIRE-BREATHING BUG.

FIRE-BREATH-ING BUG...

APPARENTLY, HE WAS KILLED BY ANOTHER ARSONIST THEY CALL "FIRE-BREATHING BUG."

!

AND ACCORDING TO IWANOME'S CONCLUSIONS, HE WAS ALSO THE ONE WHO STARTED THE FIRE IN THE SHAKUZAWA BUILDING.

STANDING BEHIND ME AND RAGING LIKE THAT ISN'T GOING TO DO ANY GOOD...

GOGOGOGO ゴゴゴゴ

I SHOULD HAVE MADE HIM SUFFER MORE...

GOGOGO (RUMBLE) ゴゴゴ

WOW.

SUPERINTENDENT GENERAL JIROUTAROU TAKANOSU.

OH, I'M SURE WE'LL MESH JUST FINE.

A GEAR... YOU SAY?

MATCHING UP MY GEARS WITH OTHERS IS WHAT I DO BEST.

...THAT'S ONLY PROVIDING NO STONES JAM UP THE SPROCKETS...

BUT...

APPEARS SO.

...YOU'RE REFERRING TO INSPECTOR MIYABI HOSOROGI.

...WHEN YOU SAY STONES...

THOUGH, I MUST SAY, HE MAY BE MISSING, BUT TO TREAT A SENIOR OFFICER LIKE A STONE...

LOOKS LIKE I HIT THE NAIL ON THE HEAD...

KO

KO
(CLAK)

HOSOROGI-KUN WAS WORTH NO MORE THAN A STONE TO YOU...

...WAS HE?

......!

HE'S NOT THE STONE.

VERY FUNNY.

SU (SWF)

GU (CLENCH)

...AND HERE I THOUGHT YOU'D SWAT MY HAND AWAY IN A RAGE...... BUT YOU'RE SURPRISINGLY COOL AND CALM.

IT'S SOMEONE RIGHT HERE IN THIS BUILDING WHO DROVE HIM INTO A CORNER.

A GREAT, BIG SEWER RAT.

BUT IT'S WHEN ONE'S WORDS AND ACTIONS ARE THE FURTHEST THING FROM COOL AND CALM THAT I FIND MOST ENTERTAINING.

...

IT SEEMS YOUR GEAR WILL BE ADDING A NEW SOUND TO THE SYSTEM.

I SEE.

IF I EVER FEEL THAT SOUND IS TOO DISCORDANT...

BE CARE-FUL.

...I'M THE TYPE THAT DOESN'T HESITATE TO CRUSH A MISALIGNED COG.

?

AH YES. AND ONE MORE THING BEFORE WE GET TO THE MEAT OF THE MATTER.

MY NAME ISN'T "JIROU-TAROU."

IT'S "JIRO-TAROU."

PAY ATTENTION TO THE SHORT, CLIPPED "JIRO" SOUND. IT'S NOT A LONG "JIROU."

...I'LL KEEP THAT IN MIND.

AS FOR THE REASON I CALLED YOU HERE TODAY...

NOW, THEN.

I'LL KEEP THAT IN MIND TOO.

PACHIKURI (BLINK)

YOU HAVE SOME KIND OF CONNECTION TO HIM......SO I'D LIKE YOU TO TAKE CHARGE OF THE CORE OF THE JURISDICTION SIDE.

"THE PHANTOM SOLITAIRE" ...

IN LIGHT OF TODAY'S INCIDENT, IT'S BEEN DECIDED THAT THE INVESTIGATION SUPERVISION WILL BE RE-STRUCTURED.

74

SO—?

SIGN: SHINJUKU IMPERIAL NATIONAL GARDEN, SHINJUKU GATE

I'll say.

ANY MOVEMENT ON THE POLICE SIDE OF THINGS?

One of them seems to be digging through information with a clear objective in mind.

A bunch of people have tried hacking into the police bureau.

After what you went and did, sonny, there's been a whole heap of activity.

I TAKE IT YOU'VE TRACED HIM, *GRANNY*?

OOH, FASCINATING.

SIGN: OLD MAID CAFÉ AMAGURI

ばあや喫茶 甘栗

THAT GOES WITHOUT SAYING...

GASHA
(CLACK)

GASHA

GASHA

GASHA

GASHA

GASHA

GASHA

SONNY.

GASHA

IT'S...

...SHIN-JUKU.

THE HOME BASE FOR A FORTUNE-TELLER WHO JUST OPENED UP SHOP...

I SEE...

I'LL HAVE TO HAVE HIM...

...READ MY FORTUNE.

RUSTLE RUSTLE

...I FEEL SUPER-COOL AND COMFORT-ABLE.

WITH-OUT A SUIT ON...

HA HA HA HA

CON-SIDER "COOL BIZ."

A BESPOKE SUIT WITH A TRICK INSTALLED RIGHT IN IT.

SO THIS PLACE IS, LIKE, LEGIT?

I HEARD THE FORTUNE-TELLER HERE IS A BOY ABOUT OUR AGE.

AND APPARENTLY, HE'S A REAL CUTIE, Y'KNOW?

EITHER WAY, I'M MORE CONCERNED WITH WHETHER OR NOT HIS PREDICTIONS ARE ON POINT.

OH.

SIGN: IMPROVE YOUR LUCK / FORTUNES

BUSINESS WILL BE BOOMING AGAIN TODAY...

#29

THE CRAZIEST THING IS THAT APPARENTLY IT WAS A REAL HANDFUL OF A CASE FOR THE PUBLIC SAFETY DEPARTMENT TOO.

I SPENT ALL NIGHT LOOKING INTO THAT SYMBOL, BUT...WELL, I DID FIND SOME STUFF.

BY THE WAY, DID YOU LEARN ANYTHING ABOUT THAT THING?

Yeah, that's pretty much what happened.

IT WAS WHILE INSPECTOR HOSOROGI WAS PURSUING IT THAT HE WENT MISSING.

And then, just when I almost had them by the tail, I got killed and ended up like this.

SO YOU SUSPECT THE CRIMINAL WAS ON THE POLICE FORCE?

...THAT'S...

It was probably a hired assassin who killed me in this building.

And not one of the baddies I'd been going after.

I THINK WE'RE AS CAUGHT UP IN IT AS WE CAN POSSIBLY BE ALREADY.

I'M FINE, BUT...

I'm sorry. I don't know for certain who's involved, so I can't say anything more on the subject. I don't wanna get you guys caught up in my drama.

KA

KA (TAKK)

KA

I'D WORRY ABOUT KAZUKI, SHIZUKI, AND KIRI-SAN.

...IF ANY TROUBLE WERE TO BEFALL POLKA-KUN OR THE SHINOYAMA FAMILY...

Yeah. That's why I say I want you to move with caution.

KA (TAKK)

KA

KA

...I KNEW IT. HE'S PRETENDING TO HAVE GONE MISSING AND IS CONNECTED TO SOME GUY NAMED HOSOROGI.

AND CORRUPTION ON THE POLICE FORCE?

JUST WHAT ARE THESE LITTLE SCOUNDRELS TAKING ON?

SUTO (CHOPS)

TO TO TO TO

AND...... WHY DO I HEAR A PEN SCRATCHING AGAIN?

THERE ARE STRANGE PAUSES IN THEIR CONVERSATION.

I'LL BRING IT IN SHORTLY!

PA (BEAM)

XIAOYU-KUN. I'M HUNGRY.

UM...YOU MEAN THAT OFFICER NAMED IWANOME?

I was able to communicate what I needed to to the right person.

My last lingering attachment to this world...

KA
KA
KA

...is this— I want this case to be left with him. He'd been working on it with me.

SPECIAL INVESTIGATION HQ FOR ALL MATTERS CONCERNING TENA SORIMURA

HOWEVER, THE NATURE OF SOLITAIRE GIVES US NO CHOICE BUT TO DESCRIBE HIM THAT WAY.

IN CONCLUSION, SOLITAIRE "APPEARS OUT OF NOWHERE AND DISAPPEARS INTO THIN AIR."

WE KNOW THAT PHRASE OUGHT NOT BE USED CARELESSLY IN AN OFFICIAL INVESTIGATION.

OUR SUSPECT HAS A TENDENCY TO WATCH WHATEVER IT IS HE'S INTERESTED IN VERY CLOSELY.

THAT IS NOT TO SAY WE DON'T HAVE ANY LEADS.

...IF WE FOLLOW THIS SYMBOL...

...CHANCES ARE WE'LL CROSS PATHS WITH SOLITAIRE.

IN OTHER WORDS, SINCE WHAT HE'S AFTER IS THIS SYMBOL...

GON CTHNKO

84

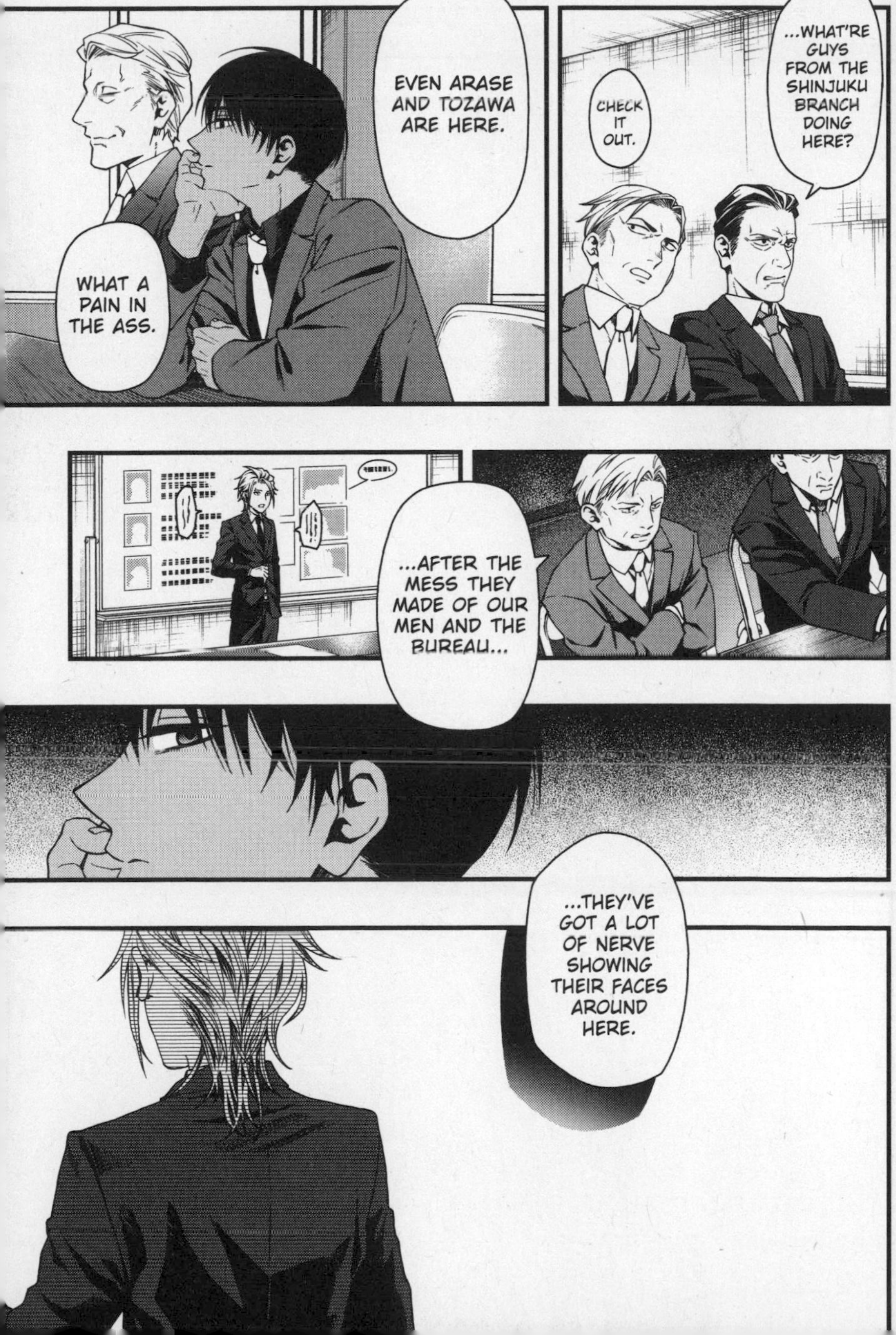
...WHAT'RE GUYS FROM THE SHINJUKU BRANCH DOING HERE?
CHECK IT OUT.
EVEN ARASE AND TOZAWA ARE HERE.
WHAT A PAIN IN THE ASS.
...AFTER THE MESS THEY MADE OF OUR MEN AND THE BUREAU...
...THEY'VE GOT A LOT OF NERVE SHOWING THEIR FACES AROUND HERE.

Fortunes

...SHOUTA YAMANO-URA.

YOU'RE AT A MAJOR CROSSROADS RIGHT NOW.

...I CAN FEEL IT.

THE "SHIP" YOU'RE ON IS IN DANGER OF RUNNING AGROUND ON CORAL REEFS ADORNED IN "OSTENTA-TION."

!?

EVERY-THING YOU'VE SAID...... HAS BEEN RIGHT ON THE MARK...

YOU SHOULD FIND ANOTHER VESSEL TO BOARD BEFORE YOU SINK.

I... I DIDN'T WRITE A WORD ABOUT THAT ON THE SURVEY FORM...

...BUT FOR THE REAL SHOUTA YAMANOURA-KUN.

WELL... NOT FOR ME...

Special Explanation!

THE THREE SECRETS OF THIS OFFICE WORKER:
① HE'S ACTUALLY SOLITAIRE!
② HE'S WEARING HOLLYWOOD STAGE MAKEUP. (SELF-TAUGHT!)
③ THE REAL YAMANOURA IS YOUR AVERAGE CITIZEN WHO HAS NOTHING TO DO WITH SOLITAIRE!

FIN

THE REPORT ABOUT ACCOUNTING FRAUD AT YAMANOURA-KUN'S COMPANY HASN'T MADE IT INTO THE NEWSPAPERS YET, SO IT'S IMPRESSIVE THAT HE WAS ABLE TO LOOK IT UP IN SUCH SHORT TIME...

IT'S PROBABLY THE WORK OF THAT HACKER GRANNY MENTIONED... TAKUMI KURIYA.

HMM...... BUT THIS IS JUST YOUR AVERAGE HOT READING AT WORK.

I HEARD SUCH GOOD THINGS ABOUT YOU OUTSIDE IN THE HALLWAY.

HMM.

Fortunes

THAT'S HILARIOUS THAT YOU'RE NERVOUS ABOUT HEARING YOUR FORTUNE.

YOU THINK I FILLED OUT MY SURVEY OKAY?

UH-OH, NOW I'M ALL NERVOUS!

OOH, THAT'S WHAT I'M HERE FOR TOO.

I'VE BEEN EVERYWHERE LOOKING FOR SOMEONE WHO'S THE REAL DEAL AND NOT JUST A FAKE.

OHHH?

Fortunes

HUH? YEAH, I'M A HUGE FAN OF THE OCCULT.

ARE YOU ALSO LOOKING TO HAVE YOUR FORTUNE READ?

88

HE EVEN KNEW ABOUT MY LEG INJURY WHEN ONLY MY FRIENDS AT WORK KNOW ABOUT THAT!

...THE FORTUNE-TELLER HERE IS THE REAL THING.

THIS IS MY SECOND TIME HERE. THE FIRST TIME, I ASKED HIM QUESTIONS NONSTOP TO MAKE SURE, AND I HAVE TO SAY...

I CAN'T WAIT EITHER!

NOW I CAN'T WAIT!

WOW!

HUH? WAS SOMETHING I SAID TOO BIG A SHOCK?

MAJOR DISAPPOINTMENT

HAAH

SHOULD I LOOK AT THIS FORTUNE-TELLER AS JUST A REGULAR HUMAN...?

DO YOU HAVE ANYTHING YOU'D LIKE TO ASK?

OH WELL.

NOW LET'S SEE...

THAT SOLITAIRE GUY... SAYS HE'LL PAY THREE HUNDRED MILLION YEN TO WHOEVER UNCOVERS THE MYSTERY OF THAT SYMBOL.

I'LL BE HONEST. I'M AFTER SOME EXTRA CASH, SO......

IJI IJI (FIDGET)

しょんぼり
SHONBONI
(SLUMP)

HAAH.

RIGHT...

SOME- THING I'D LIKE TO ASK......

キッパリ
KIPPARI
(BLUNT)

NATURALLY, MY SIGHT DOESN'T REACH TO THAT EXTENT.

AH YES...

I WONDER IF YOU MIGHT BE ABLE TO DIVINE THE TRUTH BEHIND THAT SYMBOL... HA-HA...

90

......

YEAH, WELL... MAYBE YOURS CAN'T...

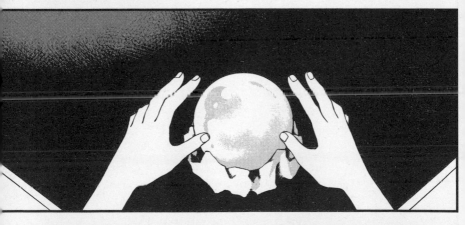

HOW-EVER...

...THERE'S SOMETHING OFF ABOUT THIS SYMBOL.

..."OFF"?

!

FUWA (FLOAT)

I WILL NOW BORROW UPON THE POWER THAT DESTINES SOULS TO WANDER THIS EARTH... TO SHED SOME LIGHT ON THE MATTER.

THERE IS AN EXCESS, SOMETHING IT DOESN'T NEED......

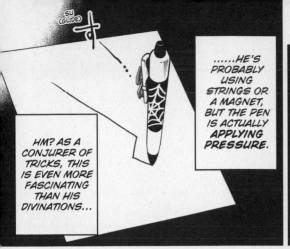

SU (GLIDE)

......HE'S PROBABLY USING STRINGS OR A MAGNET, BUT THE PEN IS ACTUALLY APPLYING PRESSURE.

HM? AS A CONJURER OF TRICKS, THIS IS EVEN MORE FASCINATING THAN HIS DIVINATIONS...

OOH... NOT BAD.

—!

...DOESN'T HAVE THE HORIZON-TAL LINE.

THE SPIRITS HAVE SPOKEN.

THE ORIGINAL SYMBOL...

I..........

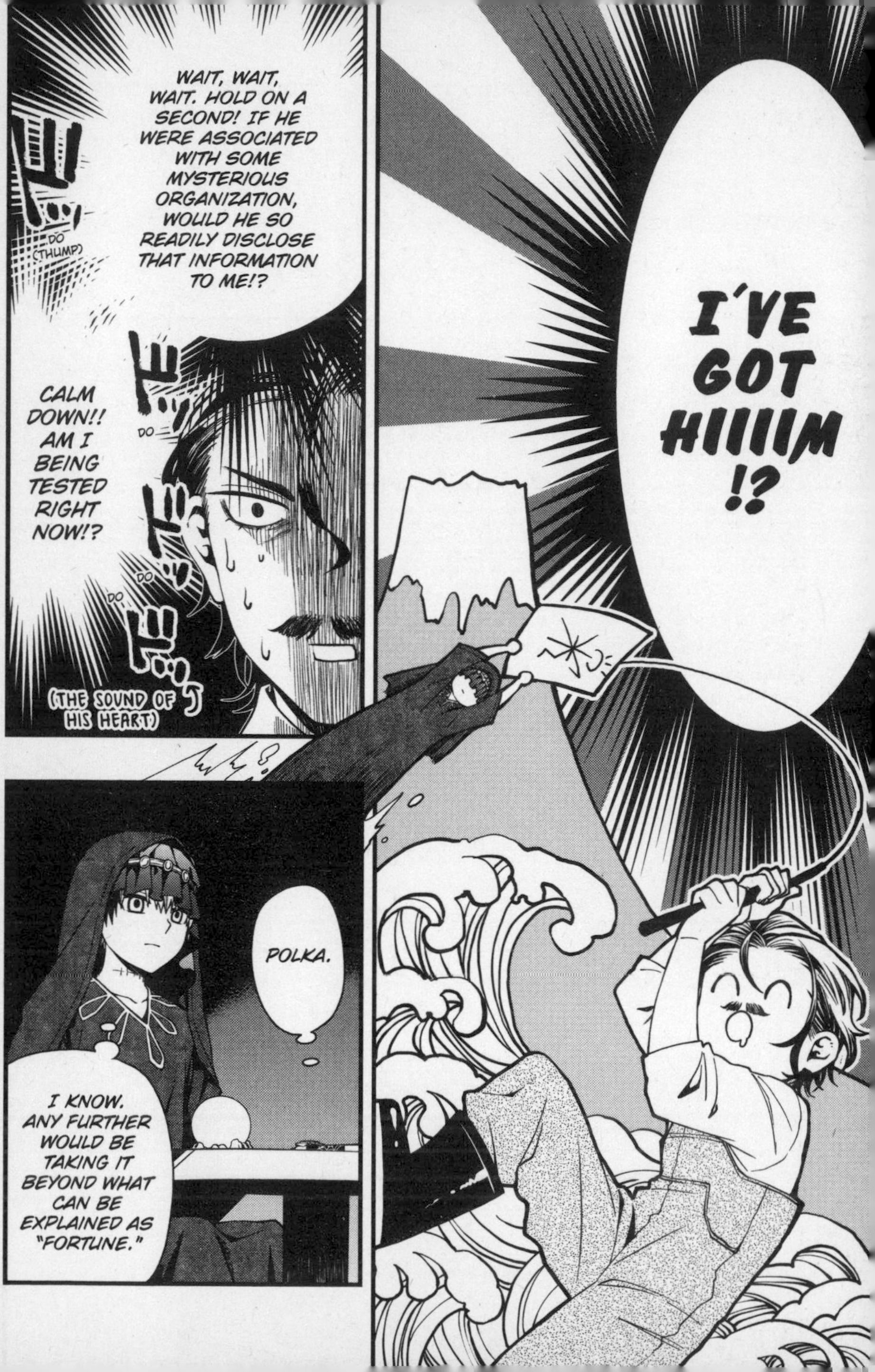
I'VE GOT HIIIIM !?
WAIT, WAIT, WAIT. HOLD ON A SECOND! IF HE WERE ASSOCIATED WITH SOME MYSTERIOUS ORGANIZATION, WOULD HE SO READILY DISCLOSE THAT INFORMATION TO ME!?
DO (THUMP)
CALM DOWN!! AM I BEING TESTED RIGHT NOW!?
DO
DO
DO
(THE SOUND OF HIS HEART)
POLKA.
I KNOW. ANY FURTHER WOULD BE TAKING IT BEYOND WHAT CAN BE EXPLAINED AS "FORTUNE."

I FEEL SICK...... LETTING THE WRONG SYMBOL BE SPREAD.

BUT...... THERE ARE SOME THINGS EVEN I CAN'T ALLOW.

OOF!

PURU (SHIVER)
!3?
3

CRITICAL HIT!!

PURU
!3?
3

TAKE THAT.

OF COURSE, UNLESS I POINT IT OUT TO SOLITAIRE HIMSELF, THEN IT DOESN'T MAKE ANY DIFFERENCE...

OH. ONE LAST THING.

I'D BEST BE GOING...

W...WELL, THEN...... I'LL REFER TO THAT.

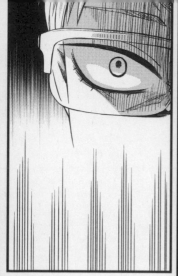

YOU WOULDN'T HAPPEN TO REMEMBER A GIRL IN A WHEELCHAIR... WHO HAD A LONG BRAID HANGING HALFWAY DOWN HER BACK, WOULD YOU?

I CAN'T TELL... WHAT SHE'S SAYING ANYMORE.

BUT I CAN SEE SHE'S WORRIED... ABOUT THE PATH YOU'RE TAKING...

SHE SEEMS INCAPABLE OF CONVERSING ANYMORE.

GU
(TENSE)

THE GHOST IS MANIFESTING THE WHEELCHAIR TOO...

THAT'S PROOF SHE'S BEEN IN IT A LONG TIME.

...THAT MUST BE MY GUARDIAN ANGEL.

HUH...THEN I'D BETTER NOT FORCE HER TO REST IN PEACE BY SENDING HER TO THE AFTERLIFE.

SU
(SWF)

IF I THINK OF ANYTHING, I'LL BE SURE TO COME TO YOU ABOUT IT.

THERE'S NO WAY HE'S A FRAUD PRETENDING AT BEING SUPERNATURAL BY USING HOT READINGS...

...MY CURIOSITY'S BEEN PIQUED, LITTLE FORTUNE-TELLER.

BATAN (SHUT)

WHAT...

...CAN HE SEE......?

HOW DID HE KNOW ABOUT HER?

HE WAS CUTE!

MAAAN, THAT WAS SO COOL!

I WAS SO SCARED!

YOU REALLY ARE JUST SO SHALLOW.

AW, IS IT RAINING?

I DIDN'T BRING AN UMBRELLA.

REALLY? THANKS!

YOU CAN USE MY UMBRELLA.

I HAVE A RAINCOAT.

MY, MY. I ENVY THE ENERGY OF YOUNGSTERS.

AWW...IT'S REALLY COMING DOWN. WHAT'LL I DO FOR AN UMBRELLA?

KNOWING AT THIS POINT WOULDN'T HAVE DONE ANY GOOD.

WE SHOULD'VE HAD HIM DIVINE THE WEATHER FOR US.

IF I GET WET, MY MAKEUP WILL RUN...

AH, IT'S RAINING.

HUH, THAT WAS SUCH AN ODD COINCIDENCE.

...I SEE. SO *YOU* ALSO ZEROED IN ON THE SAME PLACE...DID YOU?

BEING ASKED THE *SAME THING* BY *TWO PEOPLE IN A ROW.*

PASHA (SPLASH)
ぱしゃ

BUT I MUST SAY...

...THAT STYLE OF RAINCOAT YOU'VE GONE FOR...

...IS SOME-THING ELSE.

火の用心

DEAD MOUNT
DEATH PLAY

AS FAR AS HOW THE INVESTIGATION ON SOLITAIRE IS GOING...

SPECIAL INVESTIGATION HQ FOR ALL MATTERS CONCERNING TENA SORIMURA

WE'VE GOT A HUNDRED INVESTIGATORS HOLDING CHECKPOINTS ON THE STREET AND CHECKING SURVEILLANCE CAMERAS AROUND TOWN TO NARROW DOWN HIS AREA OF ACTIVITY.

BUT WE STILL HAVE NO IDEA WHAT THE MOTIVE IS BEHIND HIS ACTIONS.

KASHU (PSHT)

...MOST CURIOUS ABOUT RIGHT NOW...

WHAT HE'S...

#30

YOU GOING TO LURE HIM OUT?

BUT WE CAN'T JUST SAY SO... IS WHAT YOU'RE SAYING.

YEAH... BECAUSE WE DON'T KNOW WHO OUR ENEMIES ARE.

...VERY FEW PEOPLE KNOW THAT SYMBOL'S DESIGN IS *WRONG.*

OF COURSE, IT'S OUR JOB TO TRACK DOWN SOLITAIRE, BUT...

e garage.

s a signpost.

383 mirror.

...NOT KNOWING HIS MOTIVATION IS THROWING OFF MY HUNCH.

I THOUGHT YOU'D BE HAPPY TO HAVE MORE STAFF ON HAND TO HELP.

ONCE WE CATCH SOLITAIRE, THEN THE STORY BEHIND THAT SYMBOL WILL COME OUT.

...WHAT, SO YOU GET TO ORDER US AROUND WHILE YOU ENJOY A COFFEE?

...WELL, THANK YOU FOR NOTICING.

IT'S THANKS TO THAT I GET TO DISH OUT ORDERS TO YOU GUYS.

CRAZY TO SEE SOMEONE WHO FAILED ON HIS CAREER PATH GET PROMOTED LIKE THAT.

DON'T GET FULL OF YOURSELF.

GASHI (GRAB)

AND IF YOU HAVE TIME TO BE GRUMBLING TO ME, THEN I HARDLY THINK YOU CAN SAY I'M ORDERING YOU AROUND.

HUH... IS THAT SO?

THERE ARE TONS OF GUYS PISSED AT HOSOROGI'S HANGERS-ON LIKE YOU.

ME— I THINK IT'S TO DO WITH THAT INTERNAL AFFAIRS INVESTIGA- TION...

THE CORRUPT DETECTIVES ARE PISSED AT ME BECAUSE THEY CAN'T COMMIT BLATANT INJUSTICES ANYMORE, DON'T YOU THINK?

.......!

ARE YOU TOO SCARED TO CONVERSE UNLESS YOU PHYSICALLY DOMINATE YOUR PARTNER?

HAAH...

IS THAT YOUR PROBLEM? I KNOW BOYS ONLINE WHO ARE BETTER COMMUNICATORS THAN YOU.

DON (SLAM)

OW!

I KEEP TELLING YOU— KNOW YOUR PLACE.

IF YOU WANNA STRUT YOUR STUFF ON YOUR OWN TURF, THAT'S ONE THING, BUT HERE, YOU'D BETTER KEEP YOUR HEAD DOWN.

GA (WHACK)

WHY, YOU...

NOW, NOW.

GASHI (GRAB)

ARASE, I'M FINE.

WHA ...?

LET... GO...

MISHI

MISHI (GRIND)

MISHI

MISHI

...FINE, OKAY?

TON

I'M...

TON

I TOLD YOU.

TON (TAP)

TON

PA (DROP)

ぱっ

ARASE.

SIRS.

LET'S NOT PICK ON THOSE WEAKER THAN US... ALL RIGHT?

NI CGRIND

DON'T YOU KNOW, ARASE?

I'VE ALREADY BEEN PUNISHED FOR MY UNDER-COVER OPERA-TIONS.

OH, NO.

YOU'VE DONE ILLEGAL UNDERCOVER OPERATIONS, SO WHAT DO YOU THINK WILL HAPPEN IF YOU CAUSE MORE PROBLEMS?

I'D HAVE NO TROUBLE PINNING ANOTHER "PROBLEM" ON YOU AND—

110

AHA! THERE YOU ARE!

AND TOZAWA-SAN REALLY CHEWED ME OUT FOR IT.

ARE YOU PICKING FIGHTS HERE, IWA-SAN?

ずい
ZUI
(LOOM)

AH.

SU
(SLIP)

GURUN
(FLIP)

HUH?

Y-YEAH...
HUH?

ARE
YOU
OKAY?

BOGO
(SNAP)

HUH?

BURAN
(DANGLE)

OOPS.
CAREFUL
THERE.

BASHI
(SNATCH)

WHAT A PREDICAMENT. *YOU MUSTN'T GO DISLOCATING YOUR OWN SHOULDER* WHEN I GIVE YOU A HAND UP.

OH DEAR. IS THIS WHAT YOU'D CALL A "PROBLEM"?

!!

AND WITH THAT, THE PROBLEM'S BEEN RESOLVED.

AGH!

がコッ
GAKO (POP)

YOU'RE JUST LUCKY IT WAS WITH ME.

IF IT'D BEEN WITH ARASE-KUN, THIS COULDN'T BE RECTIFIED SO EASILY.

...IT DIDN'T TURN INTO A BIG PROBLEM.

OH, THANK GOOD-NESS...

ALSO PART OF MATERIALS COMPILING GROUP #3, FIRST-PLACE WINNER OF THE METROPOLITAN POLICE DEPARTMENT ARREST TECHNIQUE COMPETITION IN THE SHINJUKU POLICE STATION SINGLES MATCH
RANMARU YATSU

SHINJUKU COMMUNITY SAFETY DIVISION, ASSISTANT MANAGER OF MATERIALS COMPILING GROUP #3
DANJOU TOZAWA

WHAT'S GOING ON IN HERE!?

POP TOZAWA, YOU AND YOUR BUDDY SAW THAT TOO, RIGHT?

DIDN'T I LOOK COOL, PUTTING A STOP TO ARASE JUST NOW?

R... RIGHT.

NOTHING AT ALL, SIR.

WHY, IF IT ISN'T SENIOR COMMISSIONER HABAKI—

W... WE'LL BE LEAVING NOW...

Y... YES.

WE WERE ONLY GIVING "FIRST AID" TO OUR COLLEAGUE HERE WHO TRIPPED AND HURT HIMSELF... RIGHT?

IWANOME.

...WHAT JUST HAPPENED?

THEY MIGHT BE THE ONES IN THE WRONG, BUT YOU STILL SHOULDN'T PROVOKE THEM.

I GET THE SITUATION...

IS THIS ABOUT THERE BEING A TRAITOR?

EVERYONE'S ALREADY ON EDGE THANKS TO THIS VIDEO OF SOLITAIRE.

EVEN IN MY POSITION, I CAN ONLY PROTECT YOU SO MUCH.

SO PLEASE KEEP DRAMA TO A MINIMUM.

YES.

THE HIGHER-UPS ARE PROPOSING THAT THE SNIPERS WERE PART OF SOLITAIRE'S PERFORMANCE TOO.

TAKE CARE.

NOW IF YOU'LL EXCUSE ME—

I REALLY APPRECIATE EVERY LITTLE BIT OF PROTECTION YOU CAN OFFER.

HOW FRIGHT-FUL.

...IT'S STILL ONLY JUST A POSSIBILITY, BUT THERE'S A CHANCE THAT LEMMINGS AND OTHER TROUBLEMAKERS ARE INVOLVED IN THIS CASE.

PLEASE DON'T AGGRAVATE THE CONFLICT BETWEEN THE CENTRAL OFFICE AND THE BRANCH STATIONS...

...IS WHAT I'D PLANNED TO SAY TO YOU.

SO WE NEED ALL THE MANPOWER WE CAN GET, POP.

OH MY.

SAY THAT AGAIN, YATSU.

THERE'S BARELY ANY CONFLICT BETWEEN THE CENTRAL OFFICE AND THE BRANCH STATIONS, YOU KNOW?

IT'S SIMPLY A MATTER OF YOU BEING PERSONALLY LOATHED, IWA-SAN.

WHATEVER. IN ANY CASE, IT DOESN'T CHANGE THE JOB WE OF COMPS-3 HAVE TO DO.

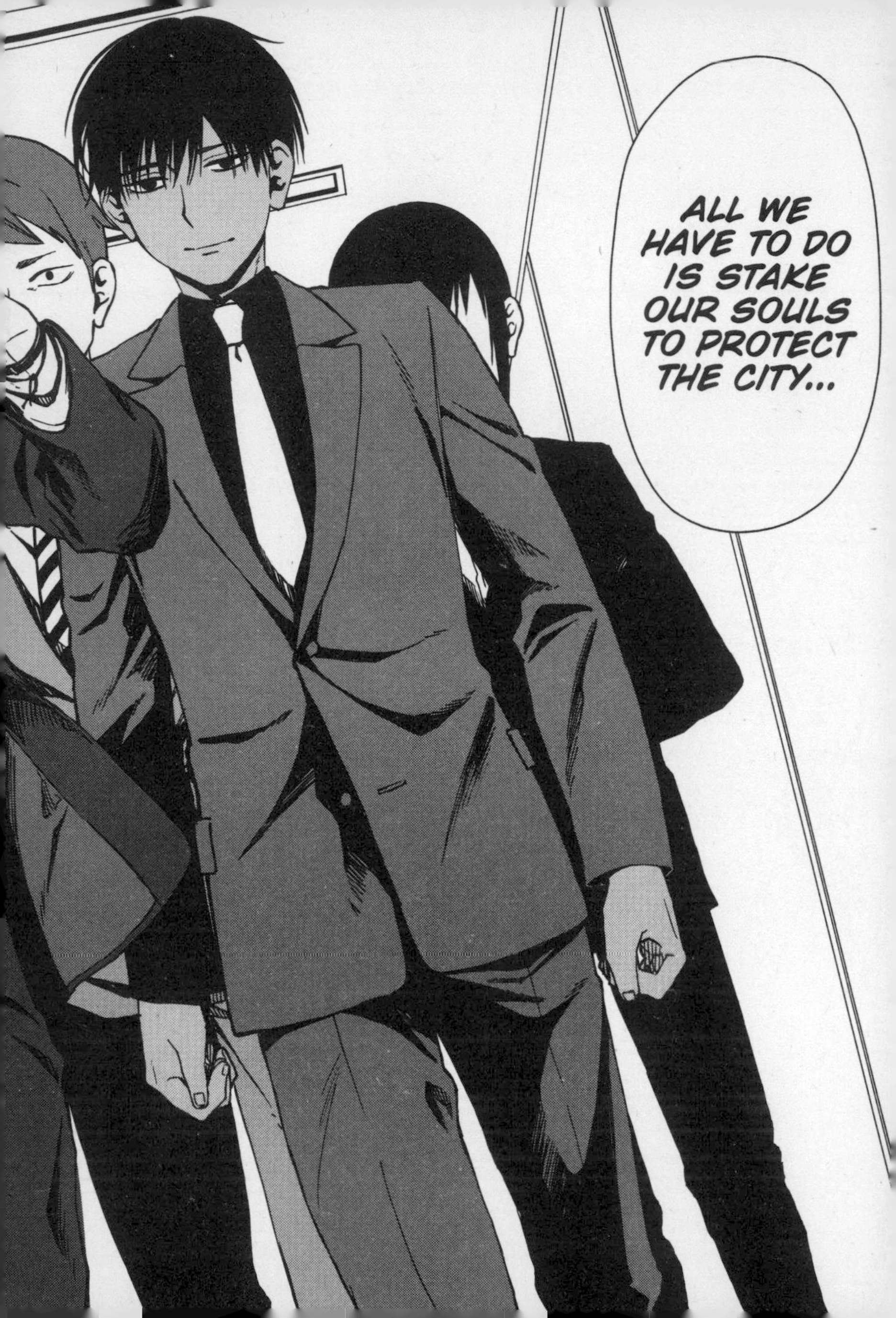
ALL WE HAVE TO DO IS STAKE OUR SOULS TO PROTECT THE CITY...

...FROM THOSE CRAZY TROUBLE-MAKERS.

SO HE'S STILL MISSING.

My beloved little brother, I was unable to track down Miyabi Hosorogi through his finances, correspondence, associates, or any other means. Also, there's a summer cold going around, so please take care of yourself. Curry keeps for a surprisingly short amount of time, so I'd recommend making it in small batches. Please be extra careful not to cause any accidents with Madam Sayo.

Your ever-doting sister,
Imbi

... HOSOROGI IS UN-ACCOUNTED FOR.

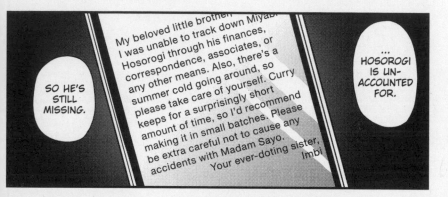

BUT...THIS BUILDING IS BEING KEPT UNDER SURVEIL-LANCE...

...BY THE MASTER'S AND TAKERU SHINOYAMA'S FORCES.

EVEN THE LEI FAMILY INFORMATION NETWORK CAN'T UNCOVER HIS WHEREABOUTS. HE MUST BE HIDING REALLY WELL.

THEN I'LL JUST HAVE TO WAIT UNTIL HE MAKES CONTACT WITH FAKE POLKA AND THE OTHERS TO NAB HIM.

STILL, I HADN'T REALIZED SHINJUKU ITSELF IS SUCH A NOISY PLACE.

I GUESS ODDS ARE LOW HE'D COME HERE DIRECTLY.

BUT THAT'S HARD WHEN YOU'RE STUCK IN ONE PLACE...

FOR AN ASSASSIN, IT'D BE EASY TO GET LOST IN THE CROWD AND MAKE A GETAWAY.

THREE A.M...

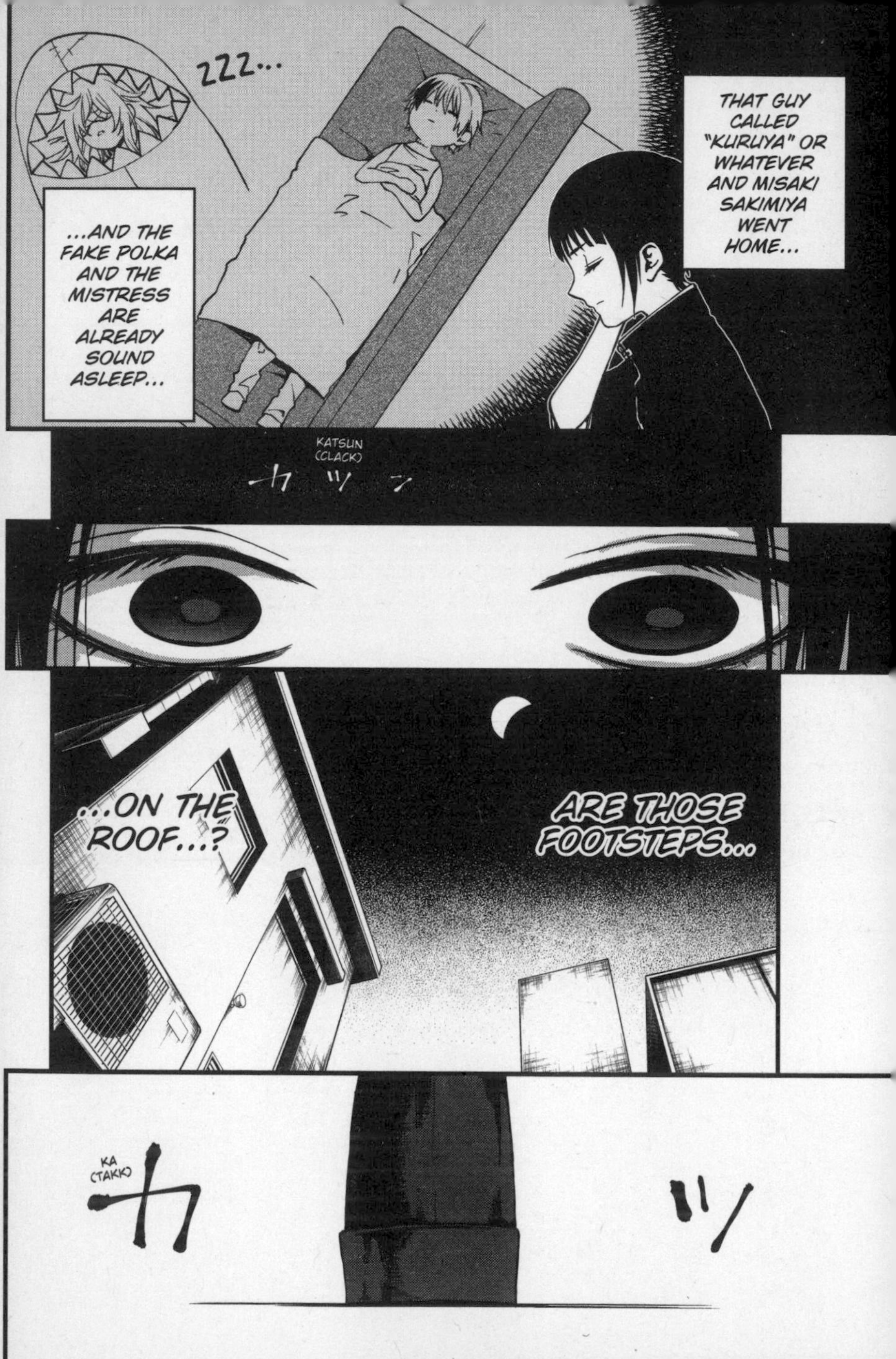
THAT GUY CALLED "KURUYA" OR WHATEVER AND MISAKI SAKIMIYA WENT HOME...
ZZZ...
...AND THE FAKE POLKA AND THE MISTRESS ARE ALREADY SOUND ASLEEP...
KATSUN (CLACK)
カツン
ARE THOSE FOOTSTEPS...
...ON THE ROOF...?
KA (TAKK)
カッ

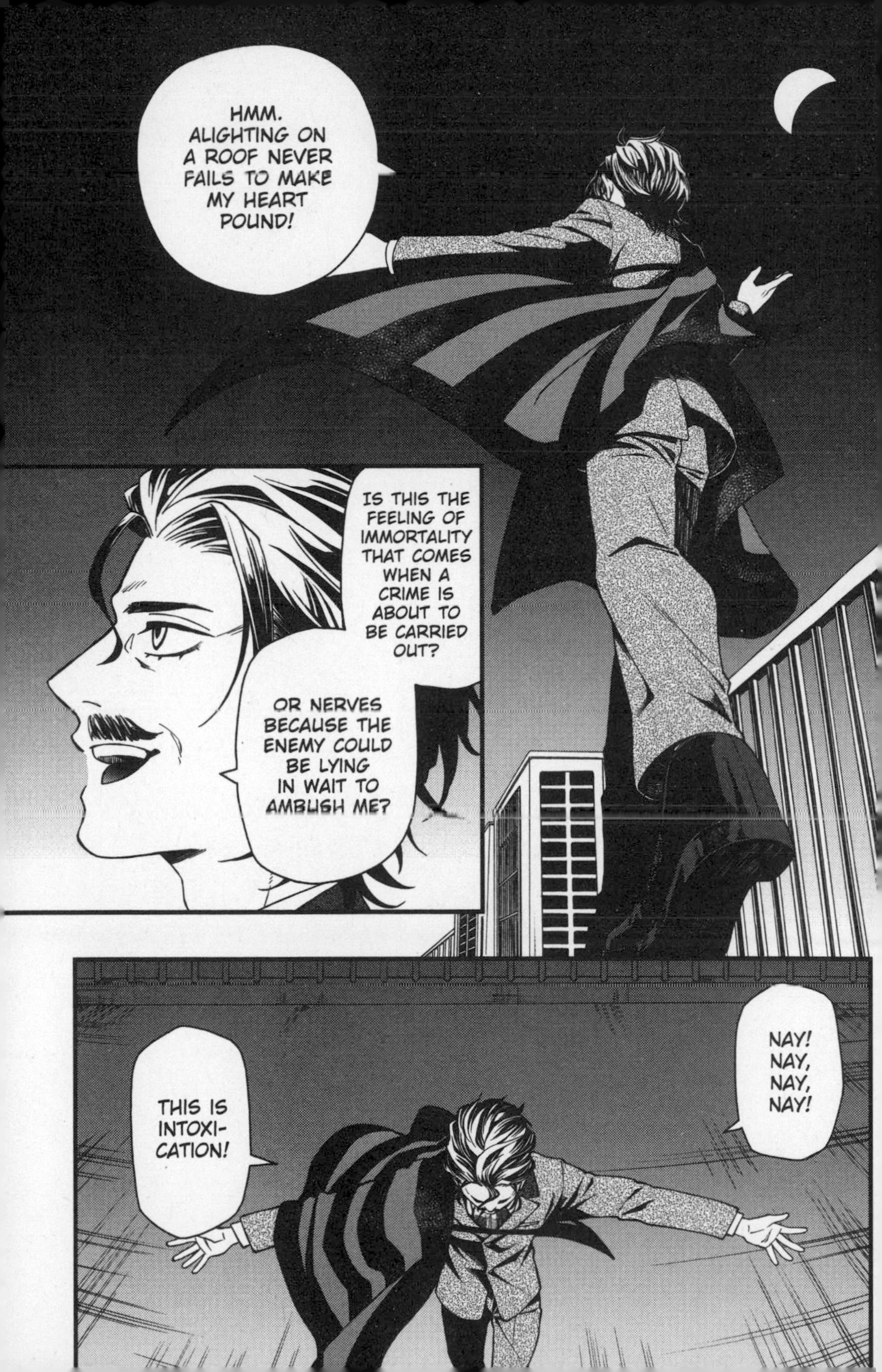
HMM. ALIGHTING ON A ROOF NEVER FAILS TO MAKE MY HEART POUND!
IS THIS THE FEELING OF IMMORTALITY THAT COMES WHEN A CRIME IS ABOUT TO BE CARRIED OUT?
OR NERVES BECAUSE THE ENEMY COULD BE LYING IN WAIT TO AMBUSH ME?
NAY! NAY, NAY, NAY!
THIS IS INTOXI-CATION!

...SO HE WOULDN'T BE MAD IF I WERE TO ADOPT THE TITLE OF "THE FIEND WITH TWENTY FACES," RIGHT?

THAT GREAT AUTHOR RANPO EDOGAWA'S COPYRIGHTS HAVE BECOME NULL AND VOID...

A MYSTERIOUS SHADOW STEALING DOWN FROM THE ROOF...IT'S THAT INTOXICATING FEELING AT HAVING BECOME LIKE A PHANTOM THIEF STRAIGHT OUT OF A COMIC OR MOVIE!

PUTTING THAT ASIDE...

THEY'RE PRETTY HARD-CORE...

WAIT A SECOND... THE RANPO FANS WOULD PROBABLY THROW A FIT...

MOYA (GLOOM)

MOYA

...WHEN I YELLED, "NAY, NAY, NAY," EARLIER...

...MIGHT PEOPLE HAVE MISUNDERSTOOD ME TO BE IMPERSONATING A HORSE?

124

WHAT DO YOU THINK?

SHUBA (FWOOSH)

LOOKS LIKE MY HUNCH WAS SPOT-ON.

WELL, WELL— WHAT A WARM WEL- COME.

GA (SHK)

KA (SHK)

KA

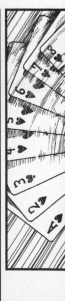

WHAT ORGANIZATION ARE YOU WITH? AND WHAT CAN YOU TELL ME ABOUT THAT SYMBOL?

SO LET'S HEAR IT, THEN!

HMPH.

...POLKA SHINO-YAMA-KUN"?

COULD YOU PLEASE NOT CONFUSE ME WITH THAT WEAKLING?

FORTUNE-TELLER "CORPSE GOD"—OR SHOULD I SAY...

WHO IS THIS!?

SOUND ASLEEP!

POLKA, AT THAT MOMENT —

ZZZ...

JIJI

PACHI (BLINK)
ぱち

ALMOST THERE!

JIJI

ジ

ZZZ...

BETA (SMAK)

JI

HYON (HOP)

JIJI

?

?

JIJI

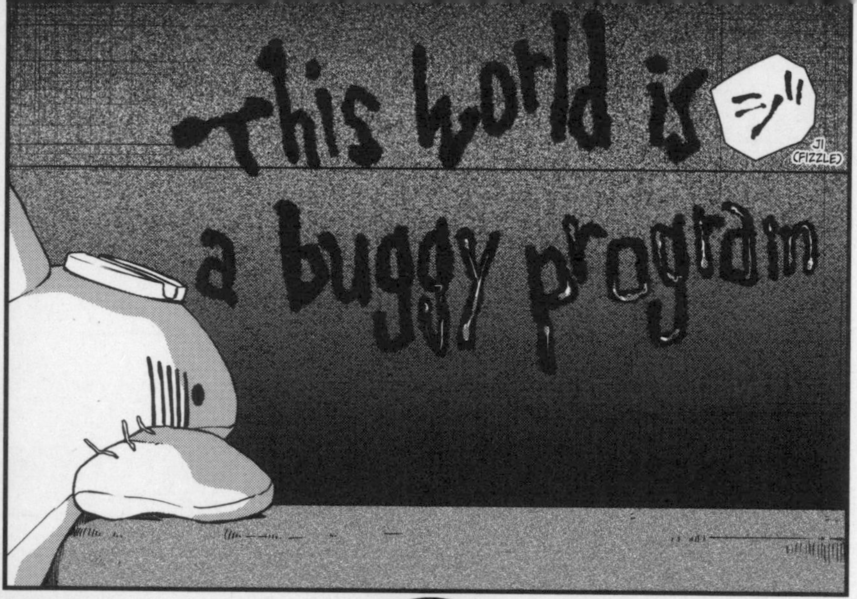
This world is
ジ
JI (FIZZLE)
a buggy program

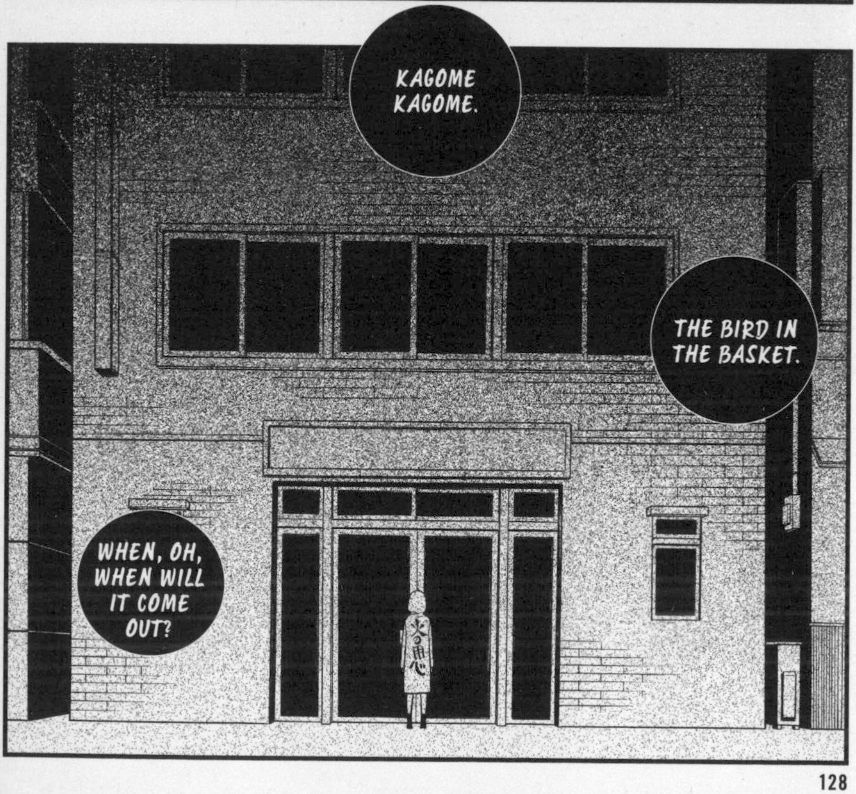
KAGOME KAGOME.
THE BIRD IN THE BASKET.
WHEN, OH, WHEN WILL IT COME OUT?

AT THE DAWN OF NIGHT...

...THE CRANE AND TURTLE SLIPPED.

WHO IS BEHIND YOU NOW...?

#31

a buggy p
Are you

JIJI
CFZZT

AND WHAT OF GENERAL DARYL!?

HE AND HIS UNIT WERE TAKEN AWAY FROM THE BATTLE BY THE HOME-WRECKER DRAGON!

HURRY!

THE ENTIRE ARMY WAS SWALLOWED UP BY A HOLE! EACH AND EVERY ONE OF THEM!

NO, THIS CAN HARDLY BE THE WORK OF ANY HUMAN!

ARE THE ANNEXED PRINCIPALITIES REBELLING!?

WE NEED TO CONTACT THE IMPERIAL GUARD...

IT RAN AWAY...!? THAT'S WHY YOU CAN'T TRUST A DRAGON...!

THE IMPERIAL PRINCE AND HER MAJESTY—

WHAT'S GOING ON!?

WHAT ARE YOU DOING, THE CORPSE GOD, MY FOOLISH PUPIL?

YOU'RE WONDERING WHY WE'RE NOT GOING?

I'VE ERECTED A PERCEPTION-JAMMING FORCE FIELD.

THE ENEMY IS ONE THING, BUT I HAVE NO INTENTION OF JOINING FOOLS IN THEIR OWN SELF-DESTRUCTION.

KA
(CLACK)

OTHERWISE, YOU AND I WOULD HAVE BEEN DRAGGED RIGHT TO THE FRONT LINES BY NOW.

THOSE OF OUR ACQUAINTANCES WITHIN ARM'S REACH I LEFT TO ROMELKA'S PROTECTION.

IT IS TIME. YOU SHOULD GET READY TOO.

...IT'S AS UTSUROJUZA SAID.

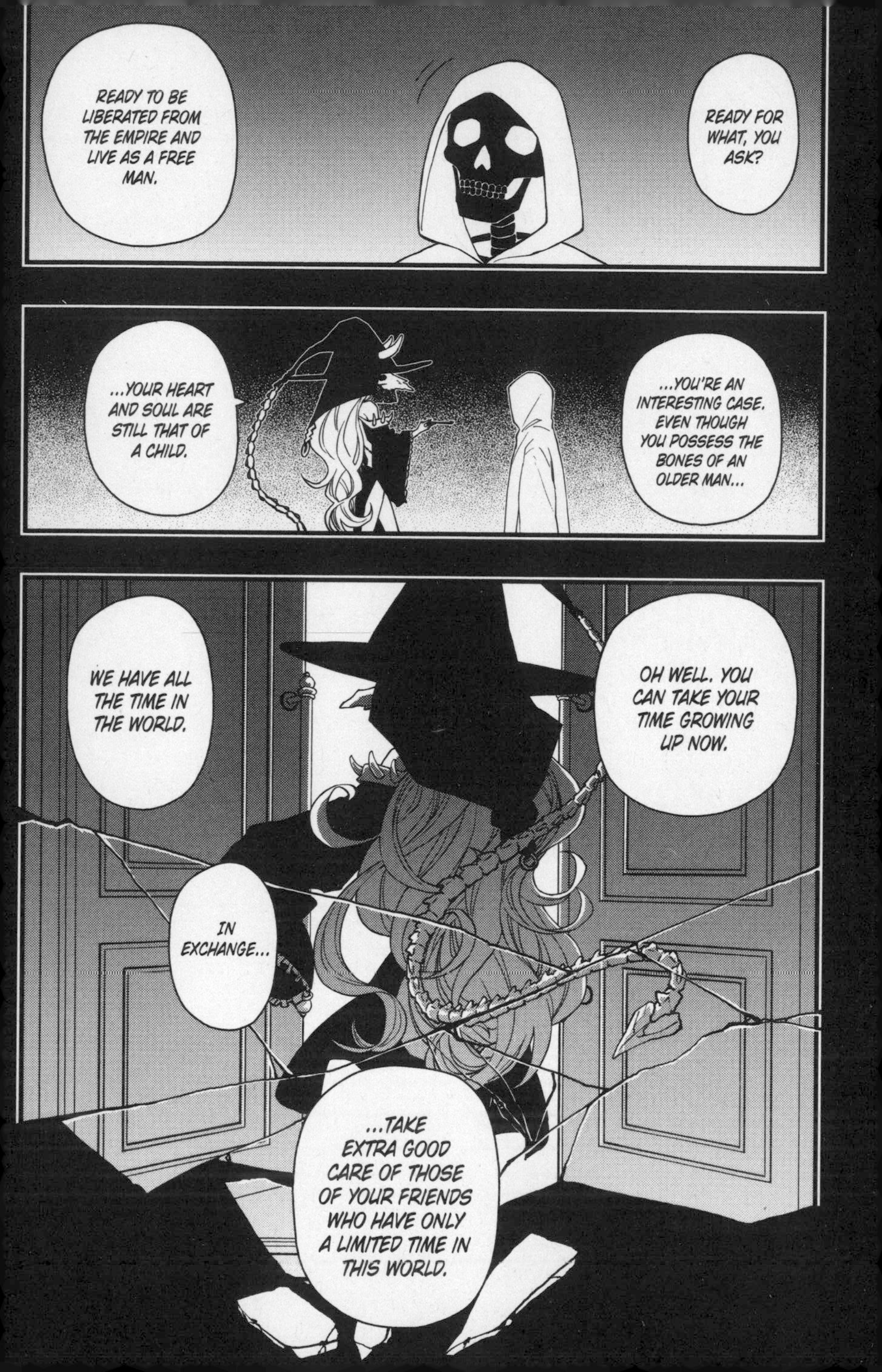
READY FOR WHAT, YOU ASK?
READY TO BE LIBERATED FROM THE EMPIRE AND LIVE AS A FREE MAN.
...YOU'RE AN INTERESTING CASE. EVEN THOUGH YOU POSSESS THE BONES OF AN OLDER MAN...
...YOUR HEART AND SOUL ARE STILL THAT OF A CHILD.
OH WELL. YOU CAN TAKE YOUR TIME GROWING UP NOW.
WE HAVE ALL THE TIME IN THE WORLD.
IN EXCHANGE...
...TAKE EXTRA GOOD CARE OF THOSE OF YOUR FRIENDS WHO HAVE ONLY A LIMITED TIME IN THIS WORLD.

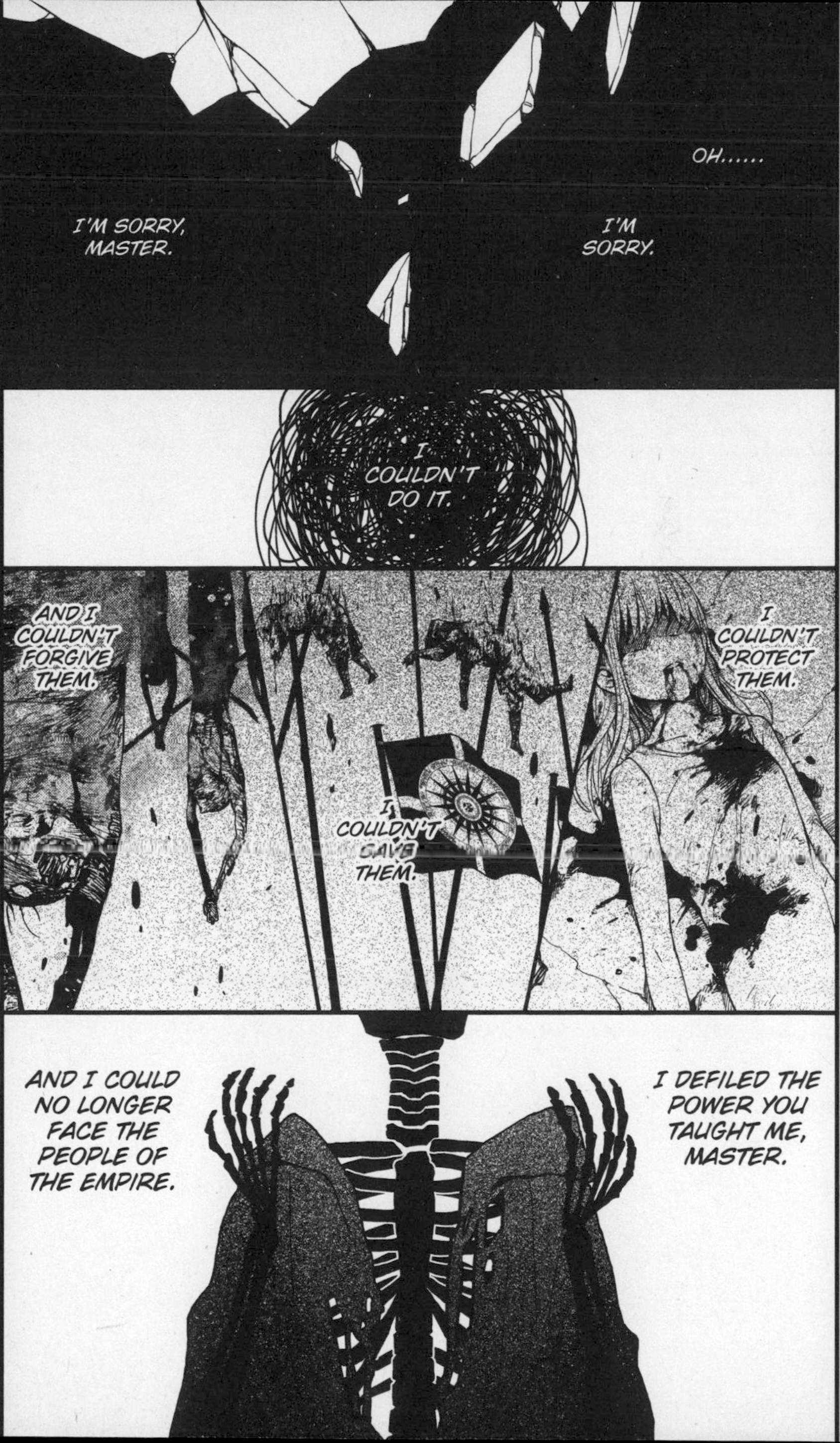

OH......
I'M SORRY.
I'M SORRY, MASTER.
I COULDN'T DO IT.
I COULDN'T PROTECT THEM.
I COULDN'T SAVE THEM.
AND I COULDN'T FORGIVE THEM.
I DEFILED THE POWER YOU TAUGHT ME, MASTER.
AND I COULD NO LONGER FACE THE PEOPLE OF THE EMPIRE.

I'D BECOME
AN ENEMY OF
THE WORLD.

SO I
FLED IT.

AND NOW, I
DON'T EVEN
KNOW WHAT
I LOVE—

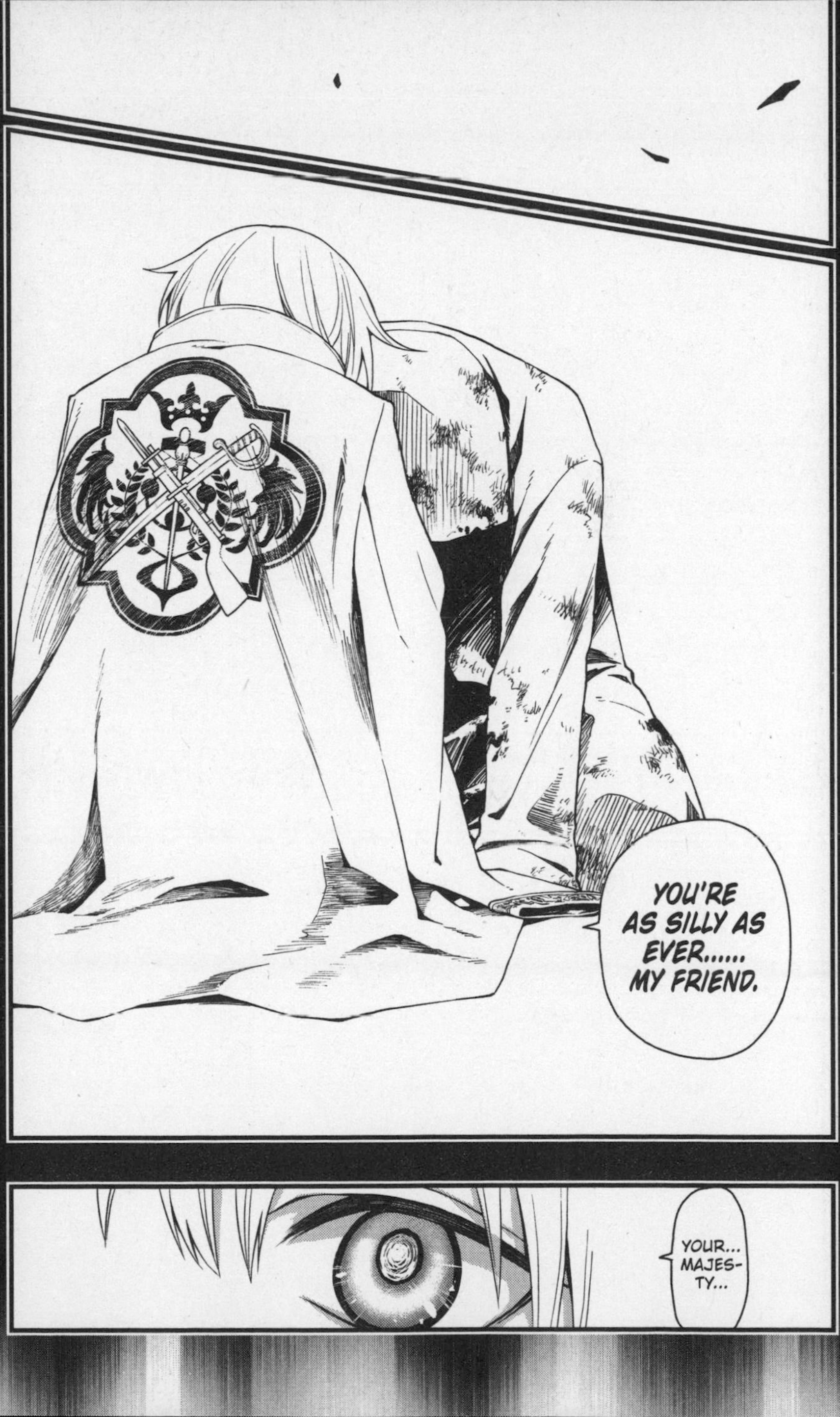
YOU'RE AS SILLY AS EVER...... MY FRIEND.
YOUR... MAJES-TY...

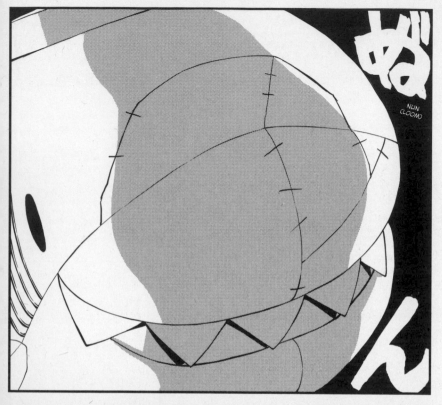

ヌ゛ん

NUN
(LOOM)

?

LOOK!
LOOK!!

WHAT'S THAT BURNING SMELL...?

ぺち WHOA!

ぺち ぺち

HOLD ON! WAIT! ぺち ぺち

I'M UP!

MUNI (MOOSH) MUNI!

むに むに

WAKE UP! WAKE UP!

べちん BECHIN (WHACK)

べちん BECHI!

!?

ス...

SU
(SWF)

136

This world is a buggy program. Are you a termite? Or are you a bird eating the bug?

NOW YOU'RE SCARED OF GHOSTS?

NO, I'D BE ABLE TO TELL IF A SPIRIT HAD DONE THIS.

IS IT A G-G-GHOST?

WHAT IS THIS...?

...WAIT— THAT'S NOT THE PROBLEM HERE.

I DON'T FEEL ANY VESTIGES OF MAGIC OR SPIRITS.

SO IT WAS BURNED USING THE LAWS OF THIS WORLD?

IT'S STILL HOT...

WHAT'S IT MEAN?

LET'S SEE...

WHO WROTE THESE LETTERS, AND WHY...?

~This world is a buggy program.~ Are you a termite? Or are you a bird eating the bug?

THIS WORLD IS FLAWED.

ARE YOU CORRODING IT? OR ARE YOU THE BIRD EATING THE BUG WHO IS?

!

PIRURURU (RIIING)

BIKU (JUMP)

?

"ARE YOU A BIRD EATING THE BUG?" "OR..."

termite

WHAT'S A "TERMITE"?

"THE WORLD IS A BUGGY PROGRAM"...?

THE SHARK IS BEING TESTED.

...HELLO.

ピルルルッ

MY PHONE.

...?

ピルルルッ

PIRURURU

ピルルルッ

PIRURURU

I DON'T RECOGNIZE THIS VOICE...

IS THIS...

...POLKA...

SHINO-YAMA?

UMBRELLA: WATCH OUT FOR FIRES

ARE YOU ALSO...

HELLO?

...WHO IS THIS?

......

...A BASTARD CHILD OF SABARA-MOND?

HOW... DO YOU KNOW THAT NAME?

HOW ...?

?

I SEE, SO THAT'S HOW IT IS.

HEH HEH HEH...

TO MAKE ME PLAY ALONG WITH THIS QUIRK OF FATE!

I MUST SAY— HOW WICKED OF *THEM*!

THIS MAN IS THE WANTED CRIMINAL EVERYONE'S TALKING ABOUT, RIGHT?

WHAT ON EARTH IS HE THINKING ...?

"THEM"...? WHAT'S HE TALKING ABOUT?

I SAID THE FIRST THING I THOUGHT OF TO TRY TO DECEIVE HIM, BUT BEYOND THAT, I HAVE NO PLAN! THINK! I NEED TO COME UP WITH SOMETHING CONCRETE ENOUGH TO JUSTIFY SAYING "SO THAT'S HOW IT IS" AND "THEM"!

I WAS WRONG!!

WHO IS THIS KID!?

I THOUGHT FOR SURE HE WAS POLKA SHINOYAMA-KUN, BUT...

HA-HA-HA! NOT SO FAST, KIDDO!

...OH WELL.

I'LL JUST INTERROGATE YOU AFTER I'VE TAKEN YOU IN.

TON (TAP)

TON

とん

とん

YOU'RE NOT OLD ENOUGH TO BE WATCHING ADULT LATE-NIGHT SHOWS.

YOU'RE STILL YOUNG.

CHILDREN SHOULD BE IN THEIR BEDS—

BESIDES, IT'S ALREADY THREE IN THE MORNING.

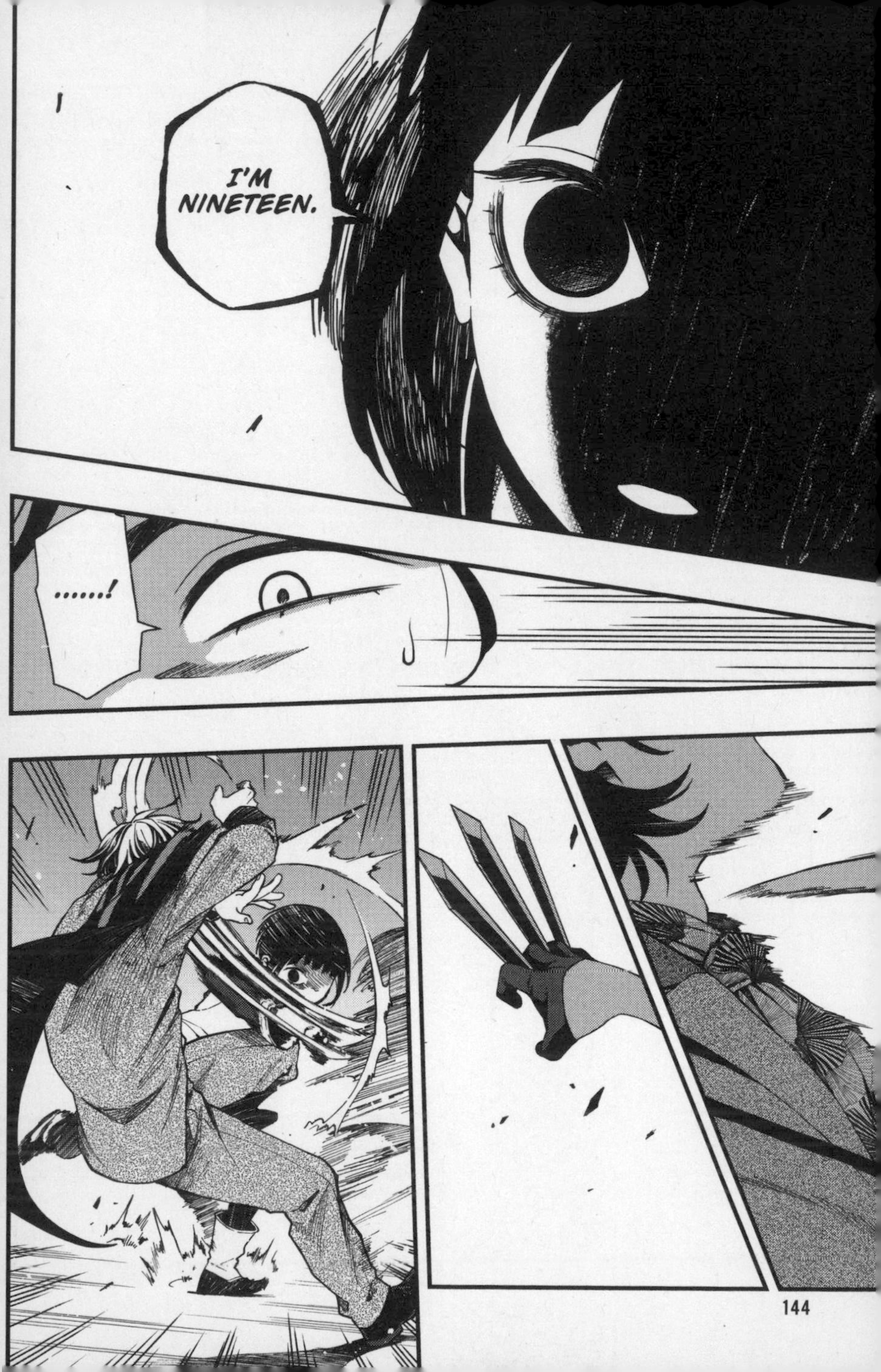
I'M NINETEEN.
......!

THOSE CERTAINLY AREN'T THE MOVES OF A CHILD.

HE'S FAST!

ZA (ZSH)

ZA

BUT NOT SO FAST THAT I CAN'T FOLLOW.

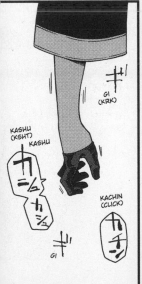

GI (KRK)

KASHU (KSHT)

KASHU

KACHIN (CLICK)

GI

...?

OOO (WHOOO)

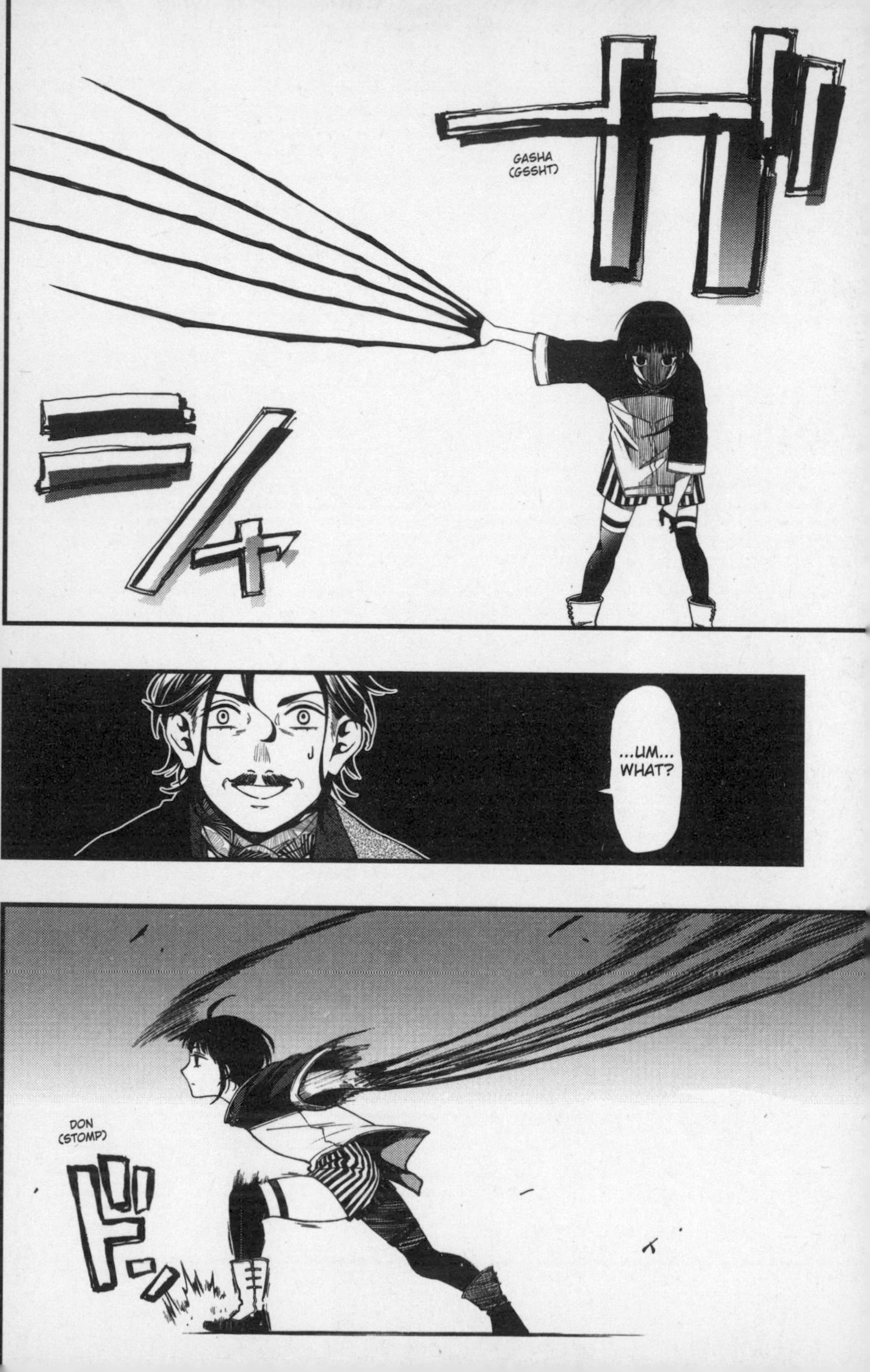
GASHA
(GSSHT)
...UM...
WHAT?
DON
(STOMP)

PYUN
CZOOM

WHAAAT!?

Prrr...

THOUGH NOT QUITE THE MOVEMENT I'D BEEN IMAGINING.

...SO THERE'S BEEN MOVEMENT.

I CAN'T BELIEVE THAT CLOWN OF A CRIMINAL IS HAVING A SHOWDOWN WITH MY OLD MAN'S PERSONAL BODYGUARD.

NOW, HOW SHALL WE USE THEIR FIGHTING TO OUR BENEFIT...?

I SUPPOSE WE'LL BE MAKING OUR MOVE TOO.

USING THE CHAOS TO GAIN CONTROL OF AN AREA...

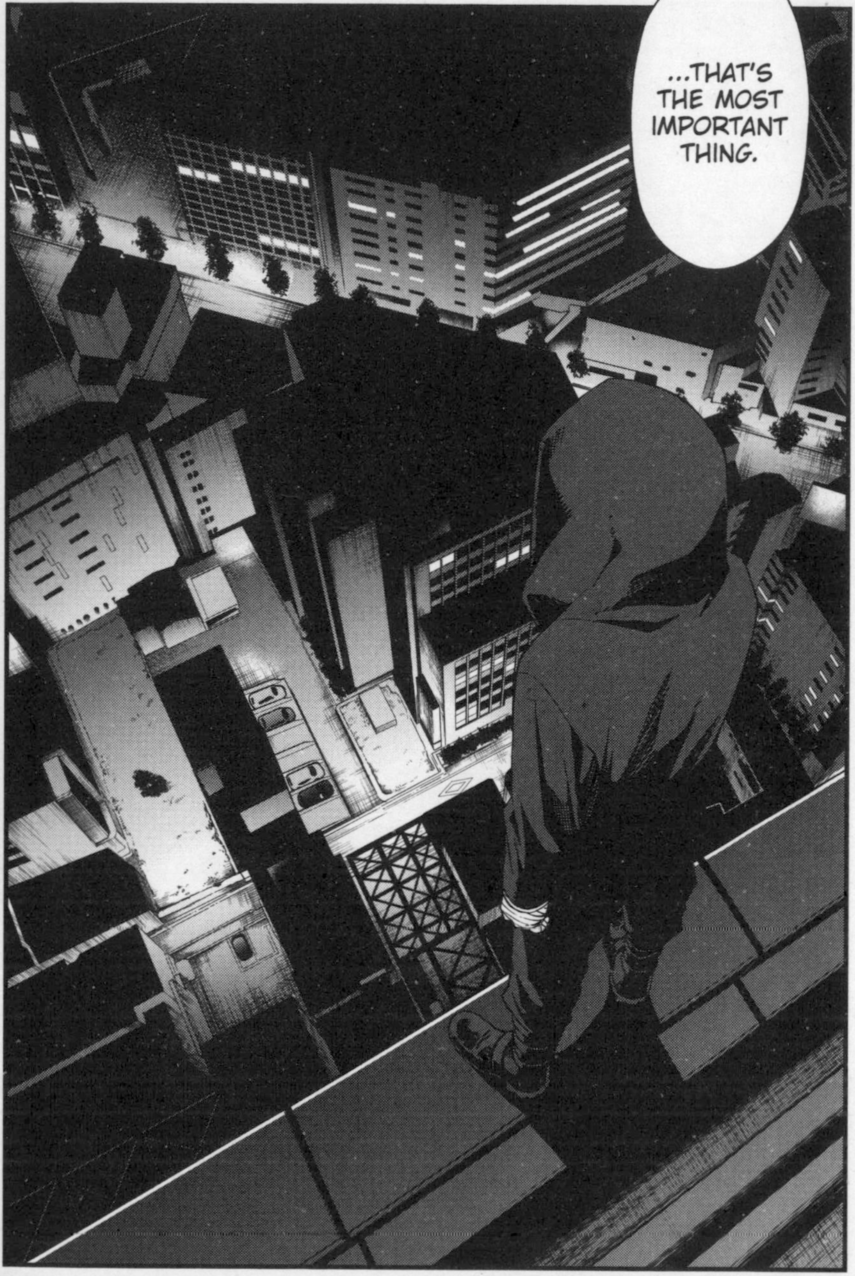
...THAT'S THE MOST IMPORTANT THING.

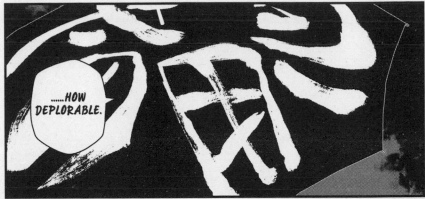

......HOW DEPLORABLE.

UMBRELLA: WATCH OUT FOR FIRES

To think they would take in...

...a child like you.

......?

#32

WHAT DO YOU MEAN BY "A BASTARD CHILD OF SABARAMOND"?

~This world is a buggy pr...m.. Are you a ...te? Or are you ... eating bug?

WHAT...

IS SABARAMOND-SAN ON THIS SIDE?

ARE YOU ALSO FROM THE EMPIRE ON THE OTHER SIDE?

OR...ARE YOU WITH THE KINGDOM OF NYANILD?

PROB-ABLY.

WAIT, NO.

IT'S PROBABLY...

...NOT THAT.

ARE YOU PLAYING DUMB?

...I... KNOW.

...THAT'S NOT A WORD...

A hostile.

No, you're one and the same.

...Are you different from them?

Polka Shinoyama, what are you?

THE LETTERS ON THE WALL WERE BURNED IN JUST RECENTLY......

AM I BEING WATCHED FROM SOMEWHERE NEARBY?

this world is program. termite? bua bird eating the bug?

......?

SHIT, NOTHING'S MAKING ANY SENSE.

154

THERE'S NOBODY ELSE ON THIS FLOOR.

THERE ARE A NUMBER OF PEOPLE AROUND THE BUILDING...

SAYO-SAN IS THE ONLY ONE ON THE FLOOR BELOW...

AND TWO ON THE ROOF...

...WAIT.

HUH?

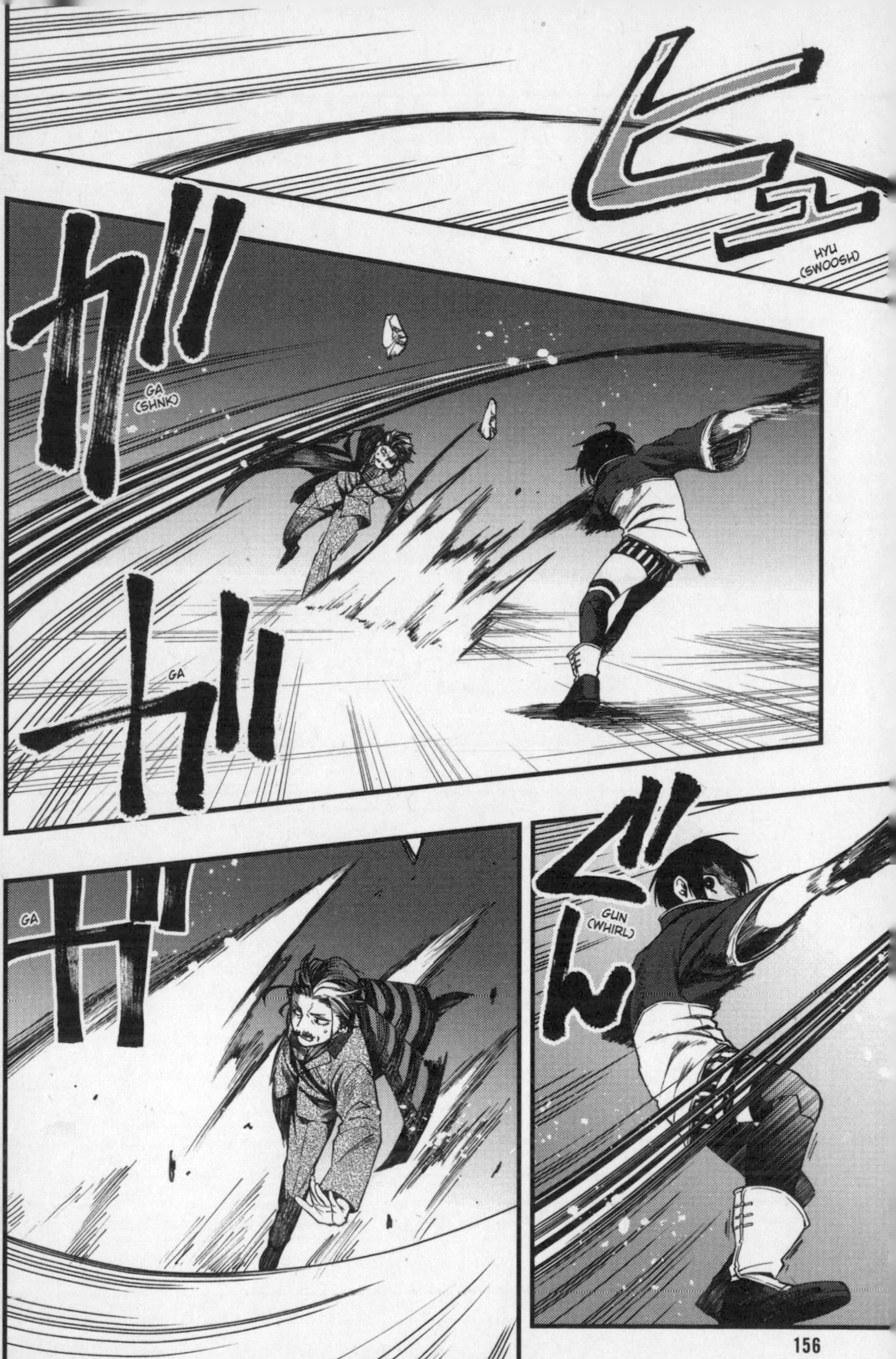
ヒュ
HYU (SWOOSH)
ガッ
GA (SHNK)
ガッ
GA
ぐん
GUN (WHIRL)
ガッ
GA

GORO (ROLL) GORO GORO GORO

HEH HEH!

ば (BA VWIP)

NOT BAD!

ALL RIGHT!! SERIOUSLY, WHO IS THIS KID? WHATEVER THE CASE, PLEASE ENABLE ME TO GET THROUGH THIS WITH WORDS, O GODDESS OF FORTUNE!!

くゎ
KUWA (SHUDDER)

ON THE INSIDE

ばくん
BAKKUN (BADUM)

ばくくん
BAKKUN

I'M SURPRISED! YOU HAVE THE MAKINGS OF A MAGICIAN, YOU KNOW THAT?

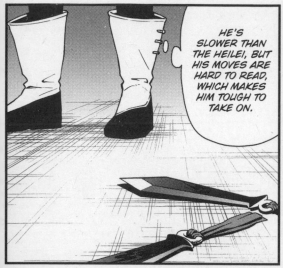

HE'S SLOWER THAN THE HEILEI, BUT HIS MOVES ARE HARD TO READ, WHICH MAKES HIM TOUGH TO TAKE ON.

WHAT'S WITH THIS GUY...?

TCH...

SHA (SHWIP)

WHY ON EARTH HAS HE COME TO SEE POLKA?

OR IS HE HERE FOR THE FAKE POLKA...?

COULD IT BE...

WHAT DO YOU WANT, OLD MAN?

I'LL ASK HIM LEADING QUES- TIONS.

158

MM!!? WELL, WELL... I DON'T KNOW WHO THAT IS, BUT I CAN USE THIS TO MY ADVANTAGE!

...YOU'VE COME LOOKING FOR SOMEONE NAMED HOSOROGI...?

HOSOROGI... YOU HAVE MY THANKS!

THAT'S IT!! GOOD LUCK, AND GOOD NIGHT, GODDESS OF FORTUNE!

I'LL REPAY MY DEBT TO HOSOROGI ANOTHER TIME!

HUH... SO YOU SAW RIGHT THROUGH ME......

VERY WELL.

HUH?

HOW COULD A WANTED CRIMINAL LIKE YOU HAVE DEBTS TO REPAY TO AN INSPECTOR WITH THE POLICE...?

YOUR DEBT TO HOSOROGI ...?

...THAT WAS ALL AN ACT, ARRANGED AND PERFORMED BY YOU?

The horror! A mysterious organization lurking in society!

MISSED

LIVE

COULD IT BE THAT WHEN YOU LET THE POLICE SHOOT YOU...

HIS HEART RATE'S INCREASED... DID I HIT THE NAIL ON THE HEAD?

I MADE THE WRONG CHOICE!! WAKE UP, GODDESS OF FORTUNE!

AAAAAH!

ZZZ...

......

...MEANT SOMETHING MUST HAVE HAPPENED TO HOSOROGI... I WAS WORRIED ABOUT HIM.

BUT......I KNEW THAT A SNIPER ATTACKING ME...

SO I CAME TO SEE WHAT IT WAS ABOUT.

MAKING SENSE OF QUANDRY

THAT SNIPER WAS ACTUALLY *AN ACT ARRANGED AND PERFORMED BY SOMEONE ELSE.*

A SHODDILY COINED PHRASE

...HA-HA-HA. LET'S JUST SAY...CLOSE BUT NO CIGAR.

......

I SEE...

NO MATTER.

ZARI (SKSH)

POLKA

OLD MAN

HOSOROGI

WHAT IS HIS RELATION TO HOSOROGI?

WELL, WELL, WELL. LOOKS LIKE YOU STILL HAVE SOME FIGHT LEFT IN YOU, EH?

...I'LL TAKE HIM IN TO MAKE HIM SPILL THE TRUTH!

WHETHER OR NOT HE'S THE MASTER'S ENEMY...

SU (SSK)

OHHH? COLOR ME CURIOUS.

BUT I WOULDN'T GO ANY FURTHER IF I WERE YOU.

YOU'LL BE IN FOR A SHOCK.

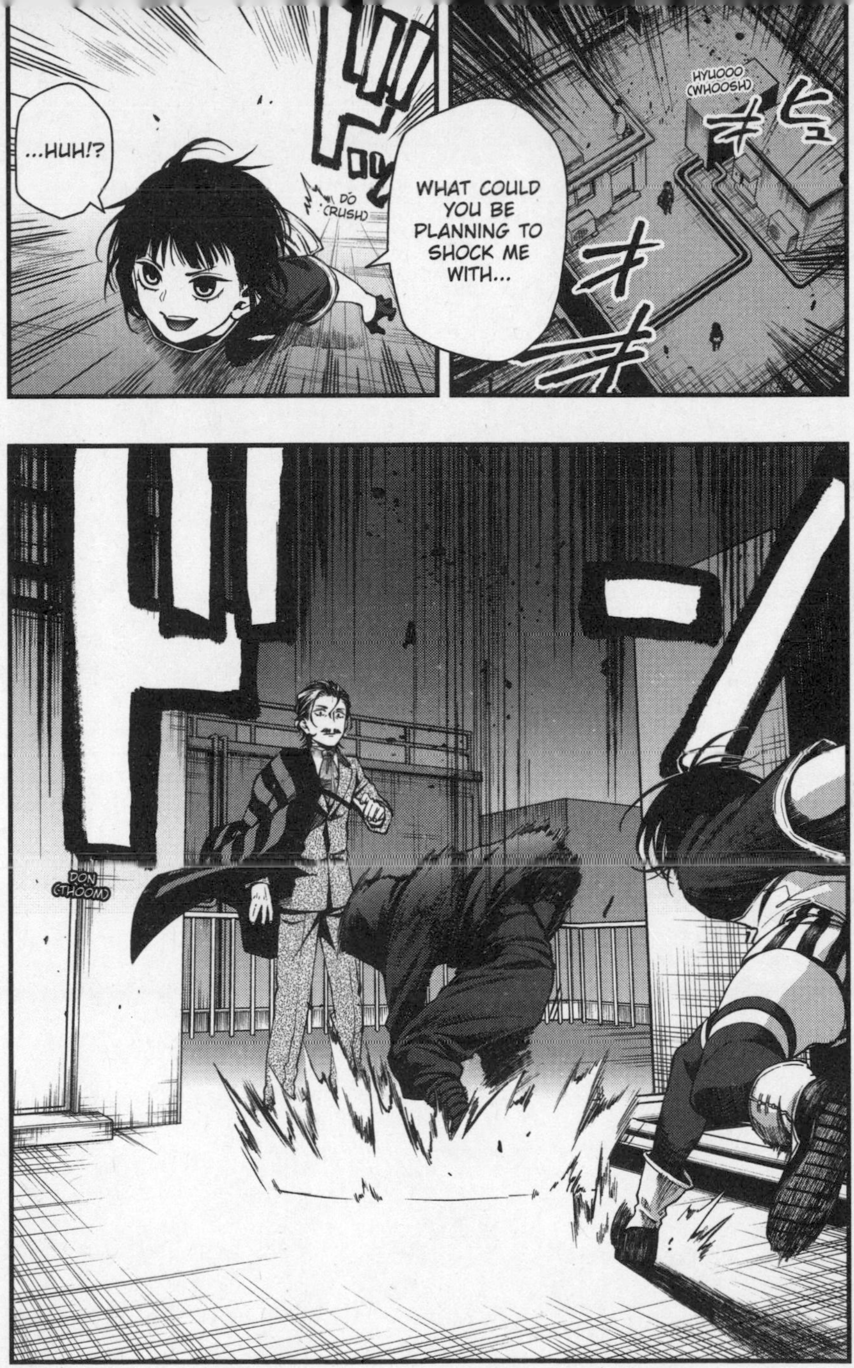
HYUOOO (WHOOSH)
WHAT COULD YOU BE PLANNING TO SHOCK ME WITH...
DŌ (CRUSH)
...HUH!?
DON (THOOM)

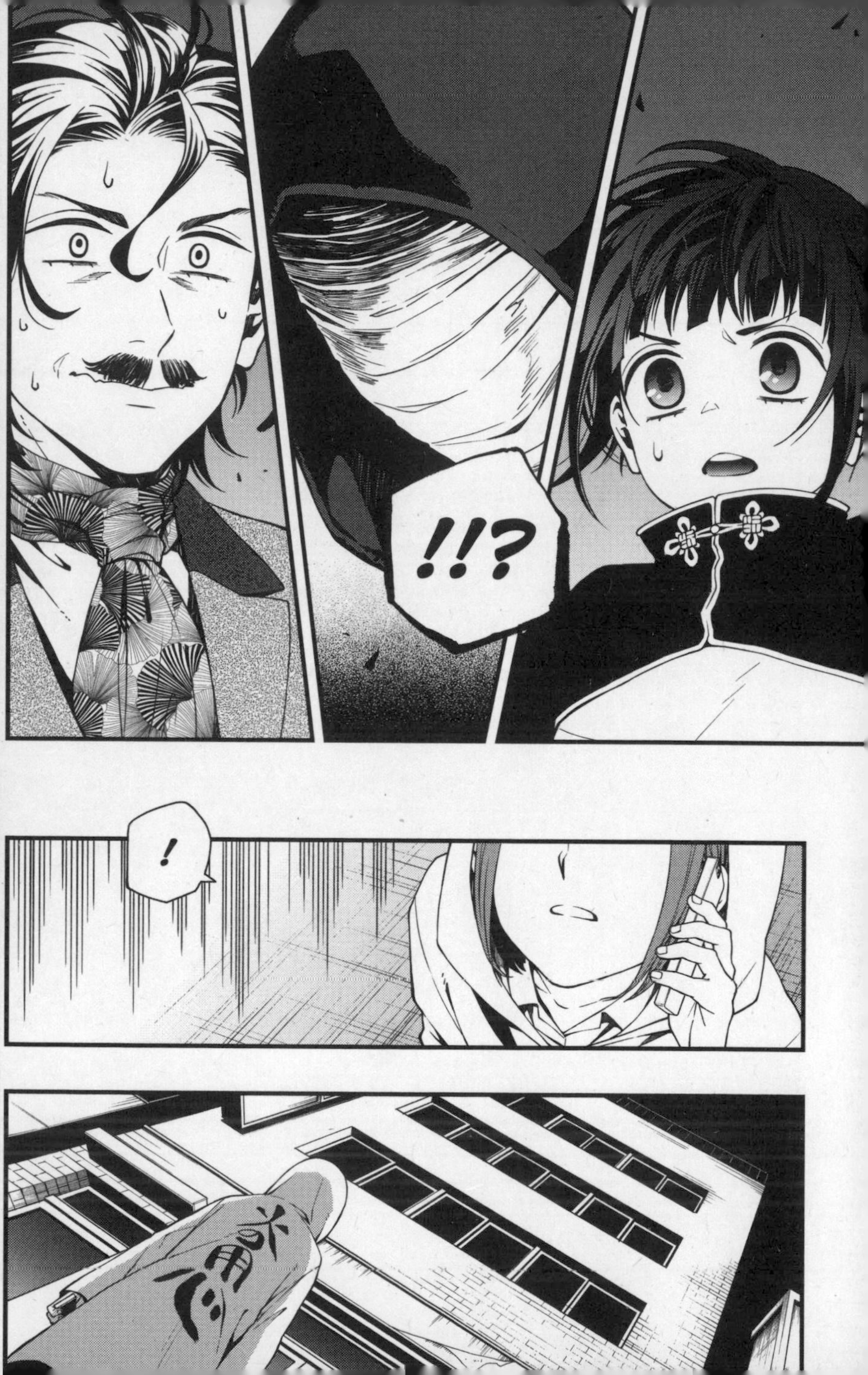
!!?
!

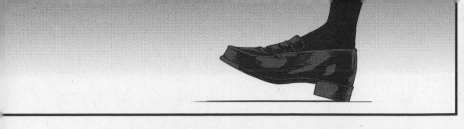

IS NOW A GOOD TIME, MISS?

UMM.

WE'RE FROM SHINJUKU POLICE STATION'S COMMUNITY SAFETY DIVISION.

DON'T WORRY— YOU DON'T NEED TO BE AFRAID OF US.

...

AS POLICEMEN, WE CAN'T TURN A BLIND EYE.

AND CHILDREN SHOULDN'T BE OUT AT THREE IN THE MORNING.

WELL...

...I'M CURIOUS AS TO WHY YOU'D BE DRESSED THAT WAY WHEN IT'S NOT RAINING...

IT'S ONLY BITS AND PIECES, BUT I KNOW FOR CERTAIN THAT ASPECTS OF MY WORLD ARE BLEEDING INTO THIS ONE.

Are you also a bastard child of Sabaramond?

WHAT'S HAPPENING ...?

WHAT IS IT?

TSUU (BOOP)

TSUU

TALKING

THEY HUNG UP...

......THE WORLD I RAN AWAY FROM......

......

...SO CORRUPTED THAT I COULD NEVER RETURN TO IT.........

I BECAME AN ENEMY OF THAT WORLD...

167

THE PLACE THAT HOLDS MEMORIES WITH ALL MY PRECIOUS FRIENDS.

DON'T SULLY IT.

DON'T TOUCH IT.

DON'T.

BASA
(SHUFF)

GIVEN THE SITUATION AND THE TIMING OF WHEN THE PHONE CALL ENDED...

...CHANCES ARE THE PERSON ON THE PHONE IS NEAR.

THAT SCARY GUY WHO MAKES THE BOGEYMAN LOOK FRIENDLY!?

THE PRESENCE BELOW IS ALSO IN A HURRY.

OF THE PRESENCES ABOVE... ONE IS UNMISTAKABLY LEMMINGS.

I'M NOT ABOUT TO IGNORE WHAT FEW CLUES I HAVE.

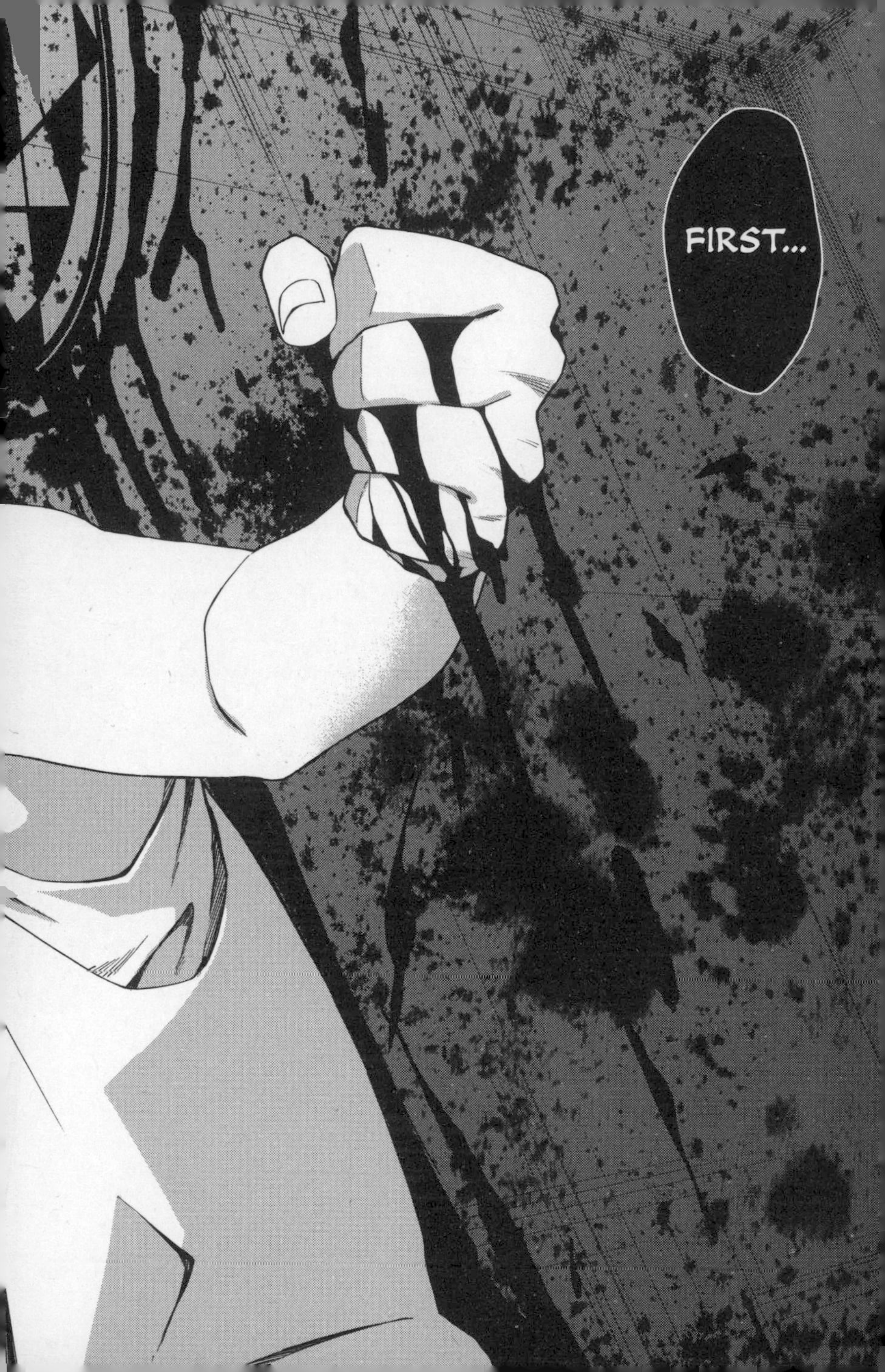
FIRST...

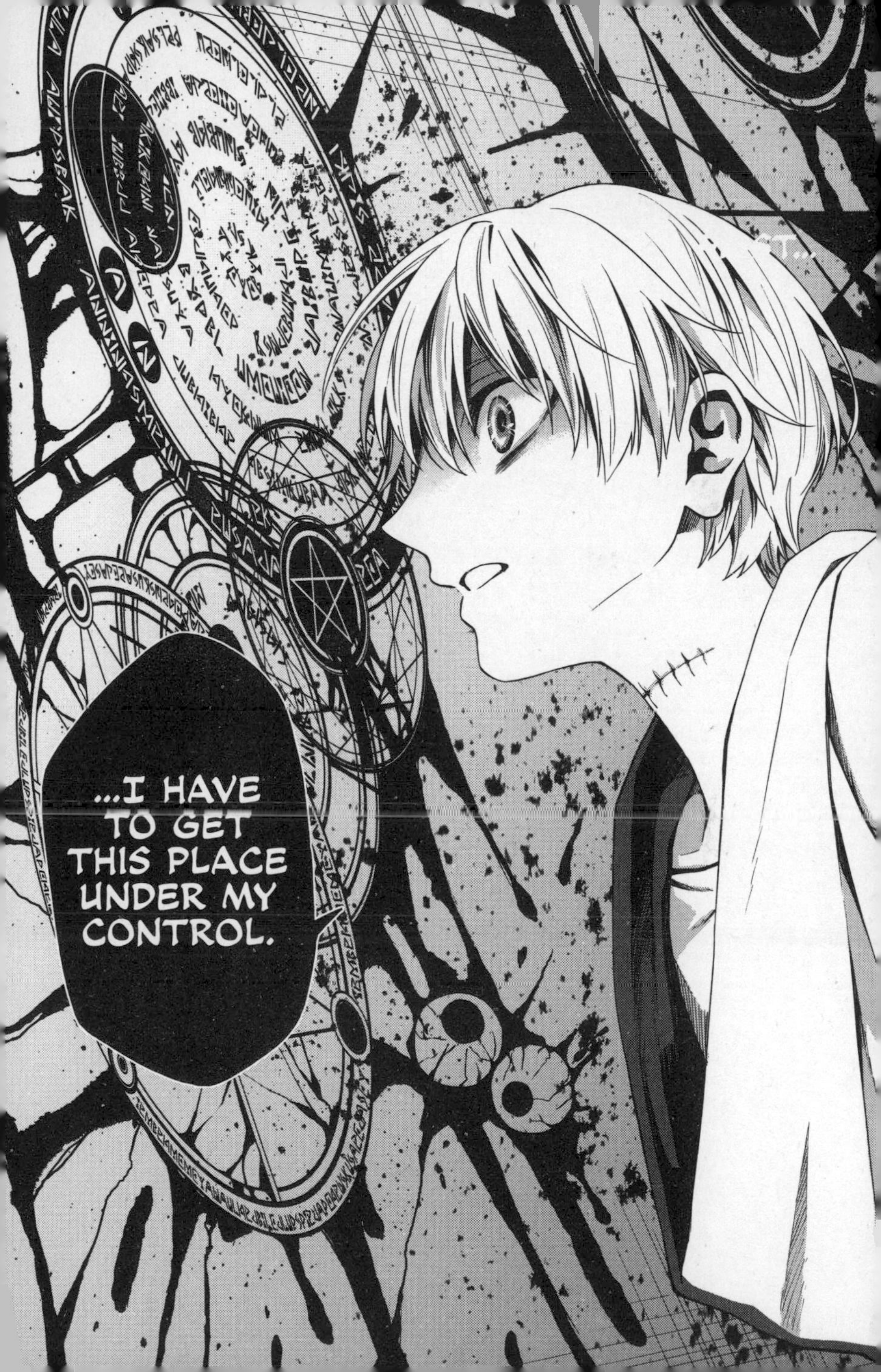
...I HAVE TO GET THIS PLACE UNDER MY CONTROL.

DEAD MOUNT
DEATH PLAY

#33

GOU
(WHOOSH)

ZURU
(SHLLIP)

SU
(SWF)

...ROMELKA?
WHAT IS IT?

ZUZU
(CREEP)

ZU

ZU

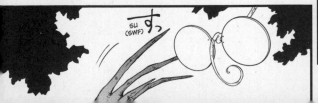

I WAS LOST IN THOUGHT.

WHY ARE YOU ALWAYS OUT HERE GAZING AT THE OCEAN, IZLIZ?

ZU
ZU
ZU
ZU (RUSTLE)

REMEMBERING A HUNDRED YEARS AGO...

...WHEN THAT ELEGANT, WRETCHED EMPIRE FELL.

FORMER SECOND-HIGHEST RANKING IMPERIAL COURT SORCERER OF BYANDY
"THE WANDERING BALCONY"
IZLIZ SWORDFLAIL

THE MOST THAT I ACCOMPLISHED IN THE EMPIRE WAS RAISING THAT FOOLISH PUPIL.

IT'S THE SAME THING.

YOU WERE THINKING ABOUT THE CORPSE GOD, WEREN'T YOU?

NUH-UH! NUH-UH, NUH-UH, NO WAY!

AND THAT'S QUITE AN ACCOMPLISHMENT!

FORMER SEVENTH-HIGHEST RANKING IMPERIAL COURT SORCERER "ROAMING WOODLANDS" **ROMELKA RIMELKA**

THE CORPSE GOD IS ONE OF ONLY A HANDFUL WHO GOT IN ON SHEER ABILITY. AND THAT HE USED NECROMANCY IN A DIFFERENT MANNER FROM YOU, IZLIZ, SEEMS TO SUIT PERFECTLY THE TYPICAL SQUABBLES YOU SEE WITH MASTER-PUPIL PAIRS. IT'S ENOUGH TO MAKE MY HEART RACE OR, MORE ACCURATELY, MAKE MAGIC RUN THROUGH THE VEINS OF MY LEAVES! I MEAN—

BUN
BUN (SHAKE) ぶん
ぶん

NOT EVERY MASTER-PUPIL PAIR GETS INDUCTED INTO THE IMPERIAL COURT'S LINEUP OF SORCERERS! I ONLY MADE IT IN AS A REPLACEMENT FOR MY OWN MASTER AFTER HE RETIRED.

MMF!

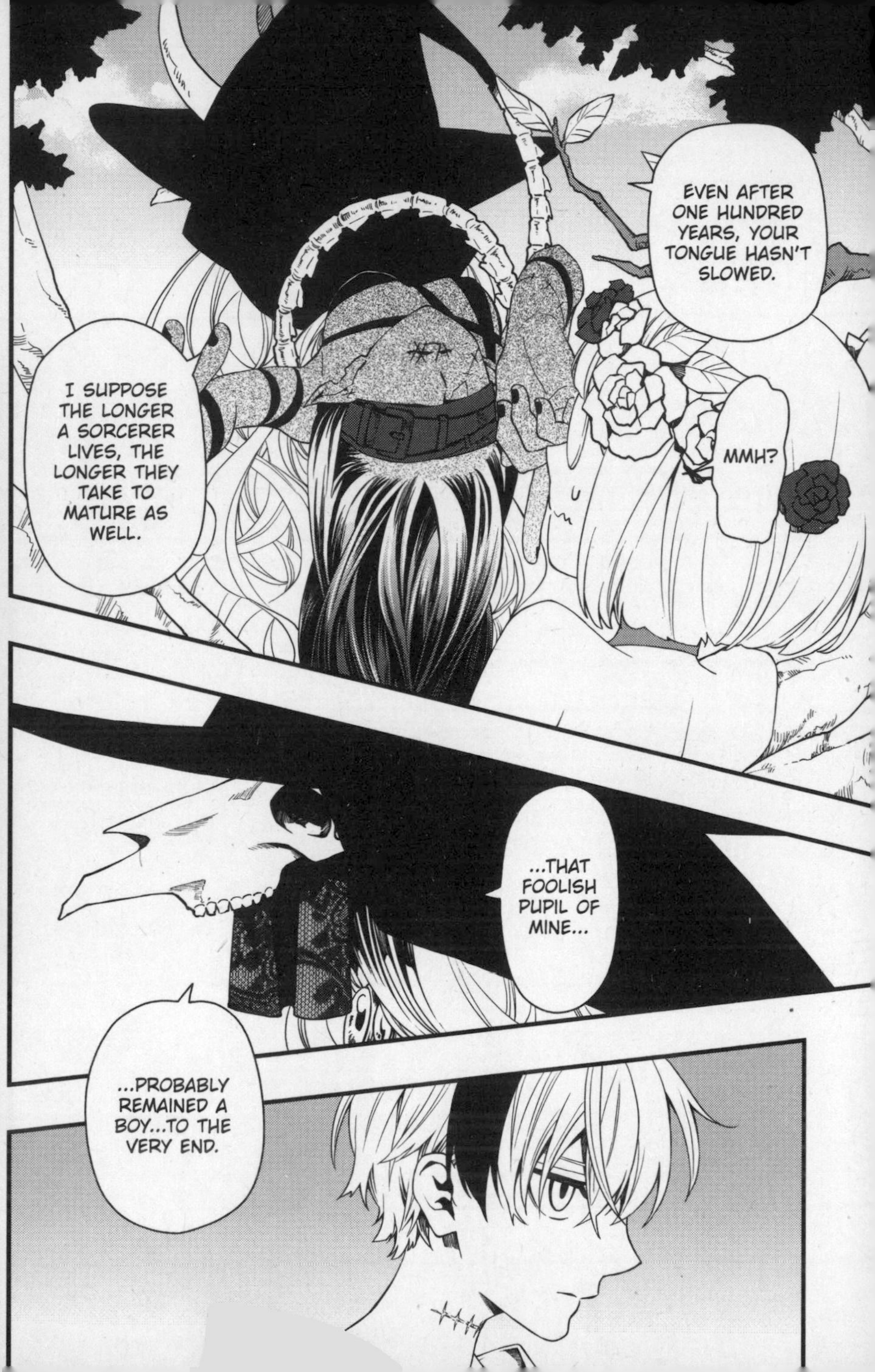
EVEN AFTER ONE HUNDRED YEARS, YOUR TONGUE HASN'T SLOWED.
MMH?
I SUPPOSE THE LONGER A SORCERER LIVES, THE LONGER THEY TAKE TO MATURE AS WELL.
...THAT FOOLISH PUPIL OF MINE...
...PROBABLY REMAINED A BOY...TO THE VERY END.

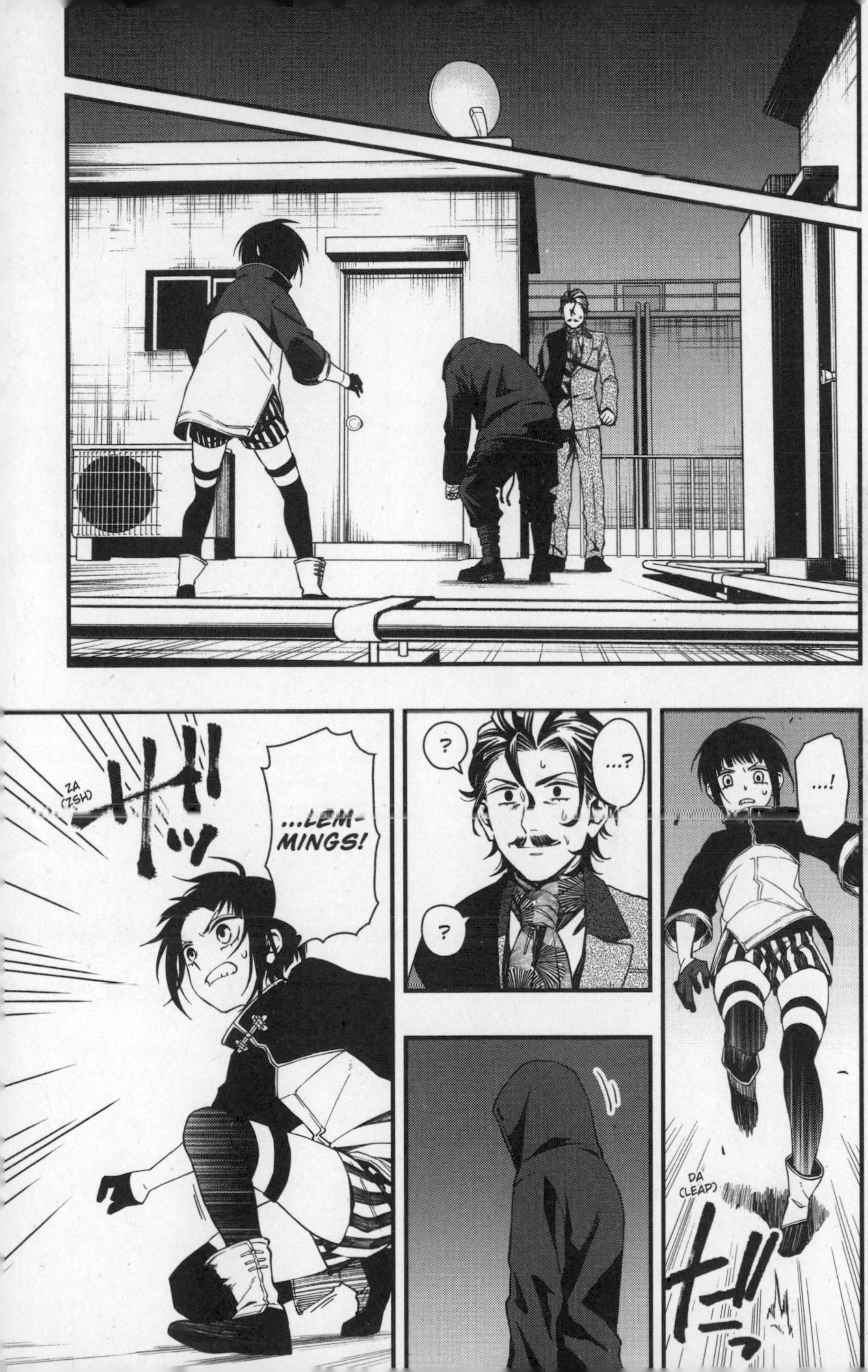
...!
DA (LEAP)
?
...?
?
ZA (ZSH)
...LEM-MINGS!

DON'T TELL ME... THIS GUY'S ALSO WITH YOU?

ONE OF THREE PEOPLE WHO MY FAMILY... THE HEILEI, WERE GIVEN STRICT ORDERS "NEVER TO INTERFERE WITH"!

THE JACK-OF-ALL-TRADES WHO'S BECOME AN URBAN LEGEND!

THE MON-STER.

HIS TRUE IDENTITY IS UNKNOWN.

HE'S A DANGEROUS MAN... EVEN I DON'T KNOW WHAT HE MIGHT DO, YOU HEAR?

AS IN, I LITERALLY DON'T KNOW HIM.

WELL, WELL! LOOKS LIKE I SHOCKED YOU, JUST AS I SAID!

THOUGH I'M SHOCKED TOO!

HEH HEH HEH...

I WANT TO RUN AWAY TOO!

WELL, THEN. IF YOU'RE GOING TO SURRENDER AND RUN, NOW'S YOUR CHANCE, ALL RIGHT?

EVASION TACTIC

BA
(WHP)

MYSTERIOUS BABY-FACE BOY, YOU DON'T WANT TO UPSET THIS BER-SERKER...

KYORO
(LOOK)

I'VE HEARD ABOUT HIM!

ONCE HE'S ON THE MOVE, NOT EVEN I CAN STOP HIM!

THE ABSOLUTE TRUTH

THEY DON'T KNOW HIS REAL NAME, BUT HIS NICKNAME'S "LEMMINGS," AND HE'S A SHREWD WHATEVER-HE-IS!

GIGIGIGI
(CRICK)

IS THIS HOW I DIE?

UH-OH.

HE'S LEAVING HIMSELF WIDE OPEN!

HYUN (ZOOM)

SHA (SWISH)

I HAVEN'T GIVEN THE FAMILY ANY DETAILS ABOUT ANYONE IN THE DRAGON KING'S PALACE AGENCY.

WHAT DO ROZAN-SAMA'S BODYGUARDS KNOW ABOUT LEMMINGS?

DON'T WORRY. WE'RE NOT ABOUT TO HURT FELLOW FAMILY MEMBERS.

THEN—

BUT LEMMINGS MAY HAVE BEEN SIGHTED AT THE FIRE.

BY MY ORDERS, HE WON'T TOUCH THEM.

I MADE IT CLEAR THAT HE IS NOT TO INTERFERE WITH MY OLD MAN'S BODYGUARDS.

...WHAT THEY DO TO HIM.

NO MAT- TER...

WHAT IS THIS GUY MADE OF...!?

...WHAT THE HELL?

CHIRA (GLANCE)

KARAN (CLANG)

GU (STRAIN)

PORO (DROP)

...DON'T YOU IGNORE ME...

IRA (IRK)

PUI (SNUB)

HYUN
(ZWOOP)

IT'S NOT CUTTING THROUGH HIM!

GU
GU
GU

GU

BUCHI
(RIP)

GUCHI
(SNAG?)

GACHIN
(SNAP)

...LET'S SEE HOW YOU LIKE THIS!

GU
GU
GU

ZURI
(SKSH)

IN THAT CASE...

バチ
BACHI

バチ
BACHI
(ZAP)

バチ
BACHI

ドツ
DO
(SLAM)

バチ
BACHI

DWAH!?

スカ
SUKA
(SWISH)

ぴょん
PYON
(CHOP)

だ
DA
(DASH)

バチ
BACHI

ドス
DOSU
(STOMP)

バチ
BACHI

バチ
BACHI

ドス
DOSU

?

!?

YOU MEAN HE ISN'T ON YOUR SIDE!?

NO ORDINARY PERSON CAN SIMPLY SHRUG OFF ELECTRIC BINDINGS AND TRY TO PUMMEL SOMEONE IN THE SAME BREATH, RIGHT!?

THAT THIS YOUNG MAN HASN'T EVEN FLINCHED AT THE DEADLY CURRENT COURSING THROUGH HIS BODY IS DEEPLY CONCERNING!

千 BACHI

ZUN

ZUN (TROMP)

バチ

バチ BACHI

ZUN

ズン

THE WAY I SEE IT, EVERYONE IN MY IMMEDIATE VICINITY IS ON MY SIDE......

ZUN

ズン

ZUN

ズン

HEH-HEH-HEH... WELL, I DON'T KNOW ABOUT THAT.

I WOULD CALL YOU BOTH "ON MY SIDE"!

AND YOU TOO, BOY!

INCLUDING THAT BANDAGED GUY!

YOU'VE BEEN NOTHING BUT A GOOF THIS ENTIRE TIME...

IRAA (IRK)

ENOUGH.

LET'S ALL JUST TALK THIS OUT!

STOP! FRIENDLY FIRE!

Please.

ZOKU (CHILL)

THIS NEXT ONE WILL *BLOW YOU BOTH AWAY.*

GASHA (KACHAK)

...

WHAT WAS...THAT FEELING JUST NOW...?

—?

...

...I WANT YOU, YATSU, AND POP TOZAWA TO SCOPE OUT POLKA SHINOYAMA'S PLACE.

HOPEFULLY, WE'RE JUST WORRYING OVER NOTHING.

LOOK, I DON'T KNOW WHAT YOU'LL FIND THERE, BUT...

THAT IWA-SAN.

...A HIGH SCHOOL GIRL WEARING A RAINCOAT EVEN THOUGH IT'S NOT RAINING...... IS A WEE BIT DISTURBING.

THE GATOR SISTERS ALREADY PROVED TO ME THAT YOU CAN'T LET YOUR GUARD DOWN EVEN IF YOU THINK YOU'RE DEALING WITH A YOUNG GIRL.

RAINCOAT: WATCH OUT FOR FIRES

I KNOW HE SAID THAT, BUT...

THE TRUTH IS, MY FAMILY'S DOG RAN AWAY...

...SO I CAME HERE TO LOOK FOR HIM WITH MY DAD.

I THINK HE THEN WENT INTO THIS BUILDING...

HMM...?

PEKO (BOW)

I-I'M SO SORRY!

DAAAAD!

OH! HERE HE COMES NOW.

TOYOMARU... HE CALLED TO LET ME KNOW HE FOUND OUR DOG, SO I THINK HE'LL BE HERE SOON.

WHAT'S YOUR DAD'S NAME?

DAD, DON'T GET MAD AT THEM.

THESE MEN SAY THEY'RE WITH THE POLICE!

WHAT DO YOU WANT FROM MY DAUGHTER?

...WHAT'S WITH THE RAINCOAT?

I FIGURED I MIGHT BE SEARCHING IN TIGHT SPACES, SO I DIDN'T WANT TO GET DIRTY.

MY APOLOGIES... I WAS LOOKING FOR THE FAMILY DOG WITH HER...

SHE AND THE MAN AREN'T TELLING THE TRUTH.

IT'S ALL WRONG.

THERE ARE NO LIVING DOGS AROUND HERE.

ONLY ONE PERSON AT THAT TIME KNEW THAT FOR SURE.

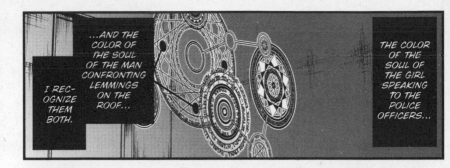

I RECOGNIZE THEM BOTH.

...AND THE COLOR OF THE SOUL OF THE MAN CONFRONTING LEMMINGS ON THE ROOF...

THE COLOR OF THE SOUL OF THE GIRL SPEAKING TO THE POLICE OFFICERS...

THAT IS NO COINCIDENCE.

WHEN I DID MY READINGS EARLIER...THEY WERE THE ONES WHO ASKED ABOUT THAT SIGIL...

THE SANCTUARY...

...WILL HAVE TO BE EXPANDED A LITTLE.

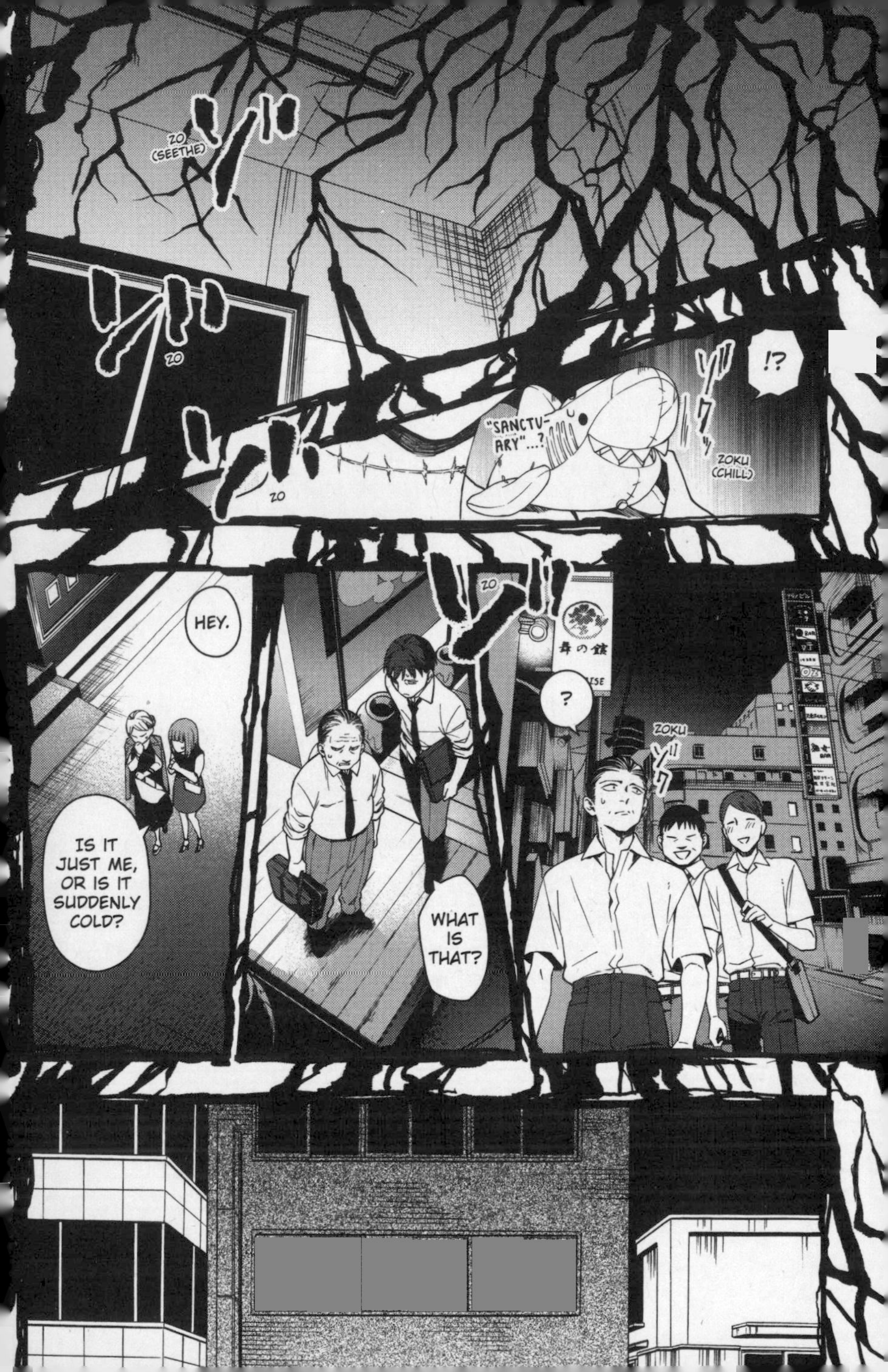
ZO (SEETHE)
ZO
ZO
!?
ZOKU (CHILL)
"SANCTU-ARY"...?
ZOKU
?
ZO
WHAT IS THAT?
HEY.
IS IT JUST ME, OR IS IT SUDDENLY COLD?

...ABOUT REMAINING A CHILD FOREVER?

AND WHAT'S SO BAD...

A GOOD CHILD.

...YES, A GOOD BOY.

HE BECOMES SOMEONE ENTIRELY DIFFERENT ON THE BATTLE-FIELD...

THE CORPSE GOD IS *USUALLY* A VERY GOOD BOY.

HUH?

BUT YOU MISUNDER-STAND.

YOU MISUNDER-STAND MY MEANING ENTIRELY, ROMELKA.

HE NEVER REALIZED IT HIMSELF, BUT... HE HAS ALMOST NO SENSE OF INDEPENDENCE.

SYMPA-THY?

SYM-PATHY.

THERE'S JUST ONE AREA WHERE MY FOOLISH PUPIL SURPASSES ME.

PERHAPS THAT'S WHY...HIS "SYNCHRONIZATION" WITH THE DEAD IS AT A HIGHER LEVEL THAN EVEN MINE.

INTEL AT A GLANCE

SH... SHE'S DEAD!?

HE DEVOTES ALL OF HIMSELF TO THOSE HE CONSIDERS HIS KIN.

THAT'S THE REASON...

THAT'S WHY.

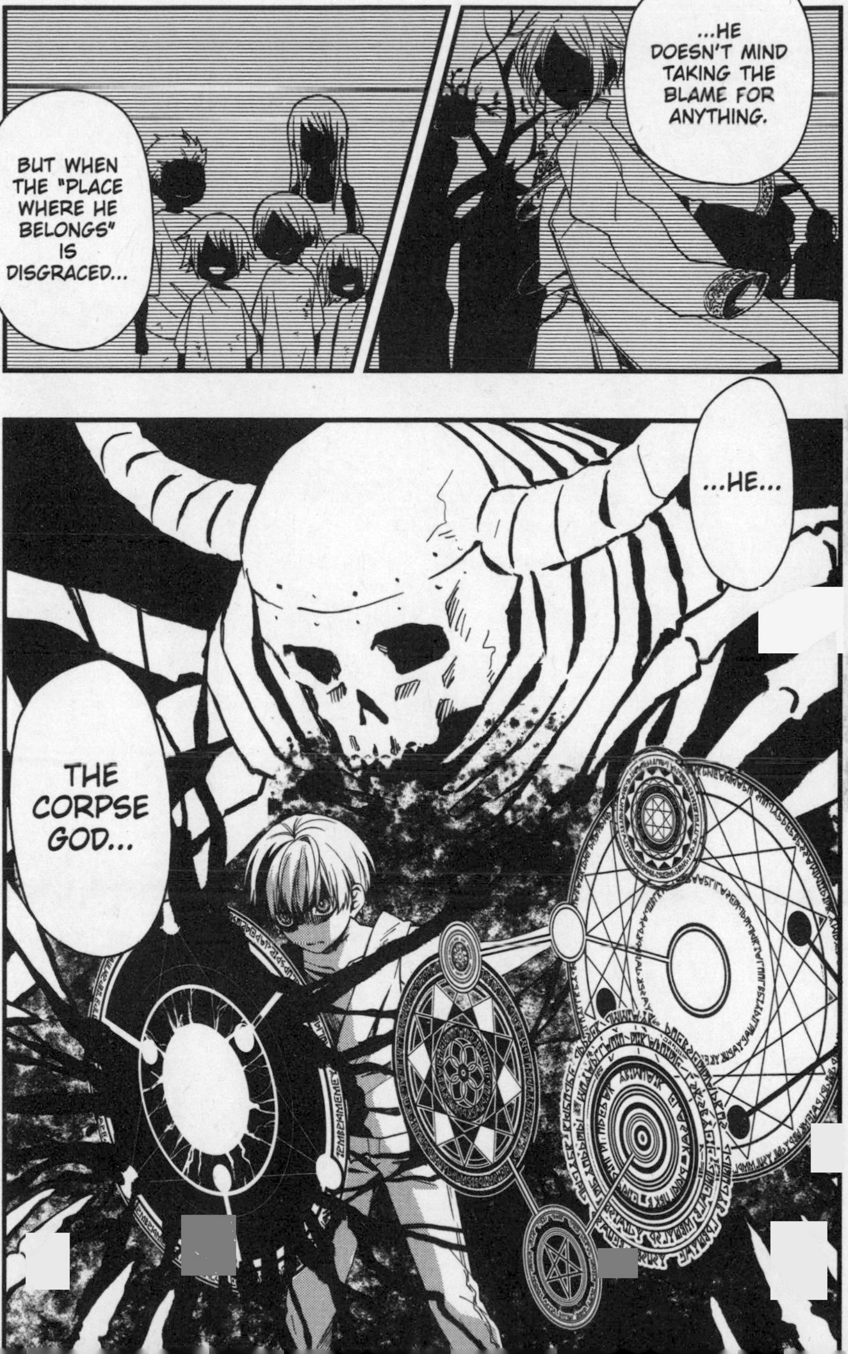
...HE DOESN'T MIND TAKING THE BLAME FOR ANYTHING.
BUT WHEN THE "PLACE WHERE HE BELONGS" IS DISGRACED...
...HE...
THE CORPSE GOD...

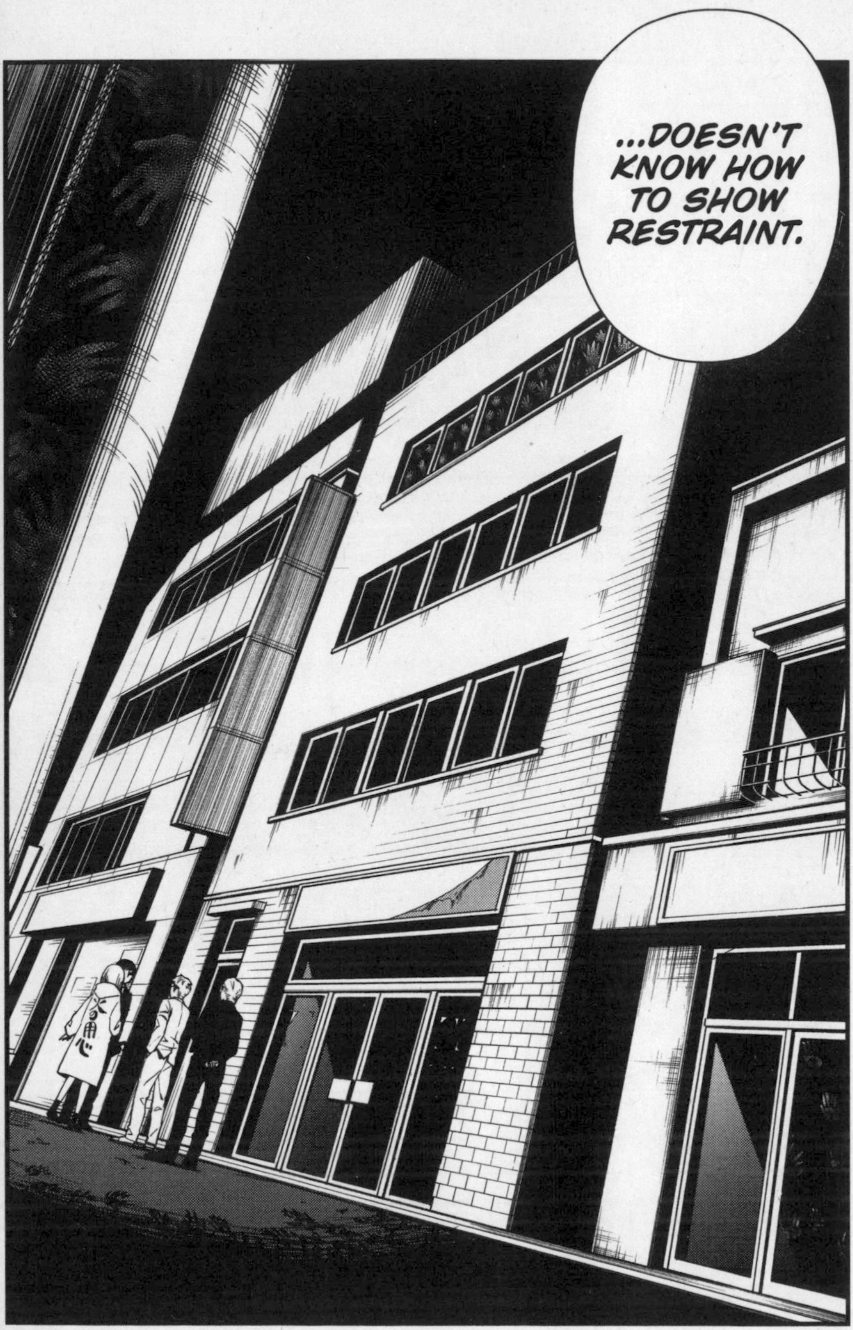
...DOESN'T KNOW HOW TO SHOW RESTRAINT.

#34

BOY, LET US REVIEW THE BASICS TODAY.

HAVE YOU EVER FOUND YOURSELF TERRIFIED BY THE WOODS AT NIGHT, SWADDLED AS THEY ARE IN SILENCE?

OR THE OPPOSITE— HAVE YOU FELT THE VERY PRESENCE OF GOD JUST BY STANDING WITHIN A TEMPLE?

ズズ
ズ
ZUZU
(SEETHE)

WE'LL BEGIN WITH THE CONSTRUCTION OF A TEMPLE.

FIRST IS THE NETHERWORLD OVERFLOW.

AND IF YOU DEVOTE ENOUGH TIME TO THE RITUAL, IT CAN ALSO BE USED IN PLACE OF A MAGIC SPELL TO CONFUSE OTHERS' ORIENTATION AND VISION.

EVEN THOSE WHO DON'T POSSESS THE EVIL EYE WILL BE ABLE TO PERCEIVE IT THROUGH THEIR OTHER SENSES.

...YOU CAN RECREATE, TO SOME DEGREE, THAT INVISIBLE, YET STILL TANGIBLE, "PRESENCE."

BY CALLING FORTH THE AIR OF "THE OTHER SIDE" AND STIRRING IT INTO YOUR OWN SURROUNDINGS OR A CLOSED-OFF SPACE...

SO THIS IS THE BEST YOU CAN DO FOR NOW.

HMM.

ZUZU
(ZLOOSH)

HNNN!

IF YOU CONTINUE TO HONE YOUR SKILLS...

SHUN
(DROOP)

THERE'S NO NEED TO RUSH, BOY.

...SOMEDAY, YOU WILL BE ABLE TO ENVELOP AN ENTIRE CASTLE IN IT.

#34

......

?

I DON'T KNOW WHAT IT IS, BUT...

MY, MY.

EVEN THOUGH IT'S BEEN HOT AND HUMID ALL EVENING.

IS IT JUST ME, OR...DID IT SUDDENLY GET COLD?

...I'M DEFINITELY PICKING UP SOME BAD VIBES.

IF THEY HAVE ANY INFORMATION, THEN I CAN'T LET THEM GET AWAY.

BUT UP ON THE ROOF AND DOWN AT THE ENTRANCE ARE THE ONES WHO CAME TO INQUIRE ABOUT THE "ROYAL EMBLEM."

LEMMINGS IS UP ON THE ROOF.

...I'D LIKE TO AVOID CONFRONTING HIM DIRECTLY.

...FIRST, I'LL ASSIST XIAOYU-KUN.

I'M...GOING TO USE AN INVISIBILITY TRICK.

BUON (VOOM)

DON'T WORRY.

BUT WON'T EVERYONE AROUND THE BUILDING SEE YOU?

EVEN THOUGH WE'RE ON A ROOF, IT FEELS LIKE WE'VE DROPPED TO THE BOTTOM OF A LAKE.

WHAT WAS THAT...? IT FEELS LIKE SOMETHING IN THE AIR SUDDENLY SHIFTED.

...BUT... SOMETHING'S DEFINITELY DIFFERENT.

I CAN'T SEE THAT ANYTHING HAS CHANGED...

HMM...... HAS THERE BEEN SOME KIND OF GAS LEAK?

SHA (SWISH)

IT WOULDN'T BE WISE TO STAY HERE TOO LONG.

KYORO (LOOK)
KYORO

JIRI (TENSE)

NO... THIS ISN'T SOMETHING PHYSICAL.

IT'S SIMPLY... YES, IT'S SIMPLY A BAD FEELING.

!?

GUSHA
(CRUMPLE)

......?

WERE EITHER OF YOU RESPONSIBLE FOR THAT?

UUUH... OKAY...I'M JUST GOING TO ASK.

ふる
FURU

ふる
FURU
(SHAKE)

DON'T LOOK AT ME.

GUN
(YANK)

SU
(STEP)

すっ...

BUCHI
(RIP)

ブチ

ZUN
(STOMP)

ズン

WHAT'S GOING ON...!?

ZO
(SHIVER)

ゾ...

GU
(STRAIN)

ぐ...

......

!?

WHAT THE...?

204

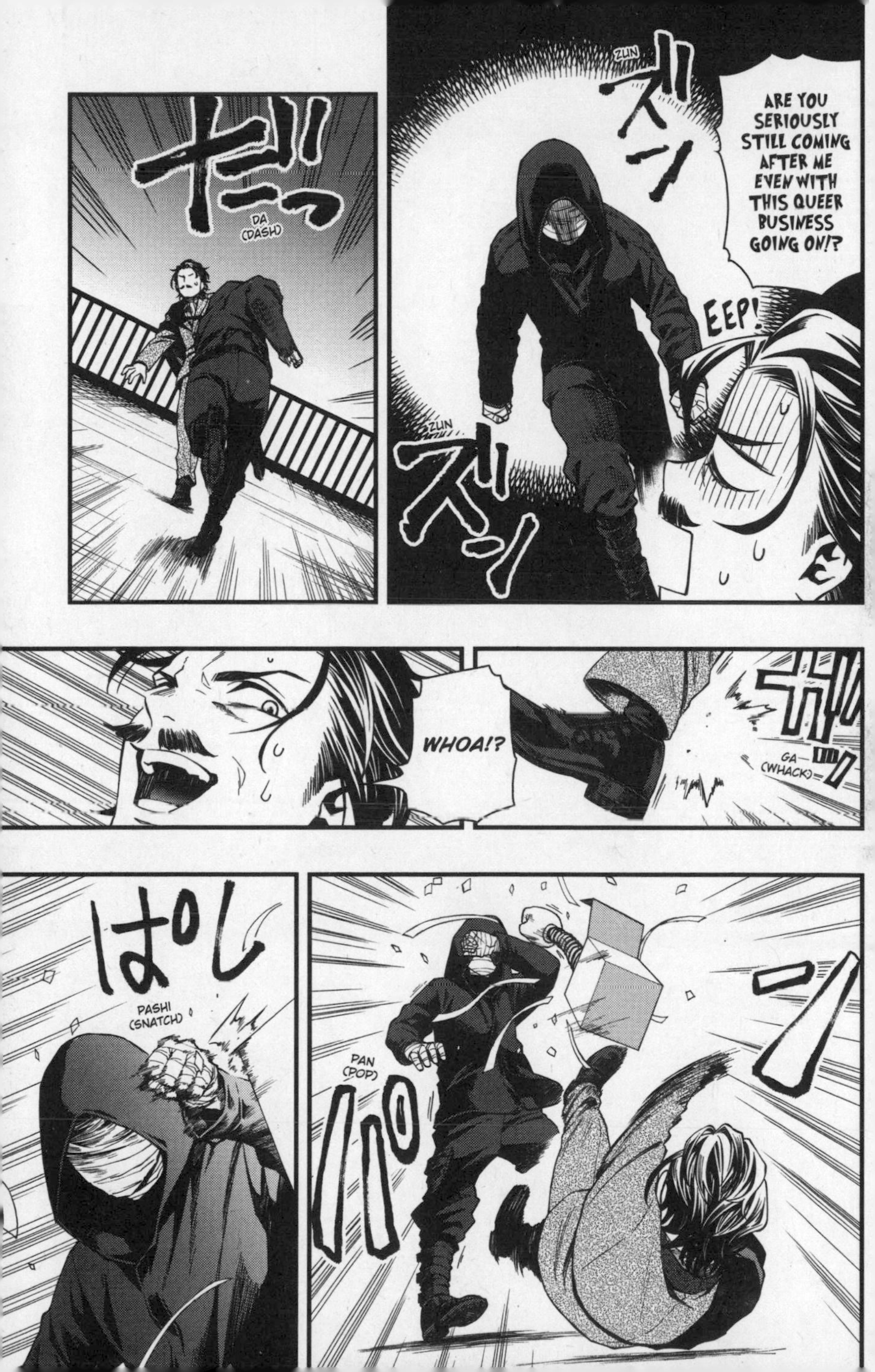
ZUN
ARE YOU SERIOUSLY STILL COMING AFTER ME EVEN WITH THIS QUEER BUSINESS GOING ON!?
EEP!
ZUN
DA (DASH)
GA (WHACK)
WHOA!?
PAN (POP)
PASHI (SNATCH)

KYORO
(LOOK)

BUSHI
(GRIP)

GUI
(YANK)

IT FEELS LIKE I'VE BEEN OBSTRUCTED BY SOMETHING FOR THE PAST LITTLE WHILE.

WHAT THE...?

WHICH MEANS, WHATEVER IT IS, IT'S ONLY COMING AFTER THE TWO OF US...!

FROM THE LOOKS OF IT, THE BOY'S TOTALLY FINE.

BY EXPANDING THE BOUNDARIES OF THE NETHERWORLD OVERFLOW JUST NOW, I'M HAVING NO TROUBLE EXERTING PRECISE CONTROL WITHIN THIS TEMPLE.

THINGS ARE GOING VERY WELL.

SYMPATHIZING WITH THE SPIRITS OF THE DEAD AND SHARING MY SENSE OF TOUCH WITH THEM REALLY IS REMARKABLY EASY TO DO.

...LET'S TAKE THINGS A LITTLE FURTHER.

ZU

ZU

ZU
(SEETHE)

ZU

ZU

SO...

ATÉ BREVE, OBRI... OBRI-SOMETHING OR OTHER!

BON
(POOF)

I'M GENUINELY FASCINATED, BUT LET'S CALL IT A NIGHT!

OH DEAR!

BON
(POOF)

!?

HM!?

GOODNESS. IT'S JUST ONE THING AFTER ANOTHER TONIGHT.

HMM! JUST AS I FEARED, IT DOESN'T FEEL AS MUCH LIKE AN ADVERTISING BALLOON WHEN IT'S JUST ME!

THAT'S ALL FINE AND WELL, BUT...

...I'M GONNA LET IWA-SAN KNOW ABOUT THIS.

UH, I'M GONNA...

SOME CHARMING ASSISTANTS TO GRAB ON TO THE ROPES!

HELP WANTED!

HERE ←

COME AGAIN?

...HOW MUCH WILL YOUR REPORT COVER?

OH...

SO SOLITAIRE'S PUTTING ON ANOTHER SHOW FOR US?

I MIXED CASSAVA FLOUR WITH RECONSTITUTED BUBBLE TEA...

THE FLAVOR OF MY SECRET SMOKE SCREEN!

HA-HA-HA! HOW DO YOU LIKE IT?

THIS... IS...

MM? WHAT HAPPENED?

I'm sending you a video clip I'd like you to take a look at ASAP.

IT'S ME.

グ
VUUU
(VRRRR)

グ
VUUU

......?

KATA (TAP)

カタ

カタ KATA

I CAN'T MAKE HEADS OR TAILS OF IT MYSELF.

WHAT IN THE...?

......

カチ
KACHI (CLICK)

WHEN THE CORPSE GOD CAME TO THIS SIDE, HE DEVISED A TECHNIQUE ADAPTED TO THIS WORLD'S MAKEUP.

THE PHENOMENON CAME ABOUT BECAUSE THIS WORLD IS SO WEAK IN MAGICAL ESSENCE.

A NEW NECROMANCY.

HOW KIND OF YOU TO USE ME AS A DISTRACTION.

SO YOU'RE HERE TOO, FIRE-BREATHING BUG-KUN.

STREET: STOP

WHY AM I SO QUICK TO FORGIVE?

BECAUSE I'M IN A SUPER-EXCELLENT GOOD MOOD AT THE MOMENT!

FINE! GO RIGHT AHEAD!

...A GREAT BRIDGE OF HOPE IS GLITTERING RIGHT BEFORE MY EYES LIKE A RAINBOW!

IT'S DIFFICULT TO BE CERTAIN, BUT...

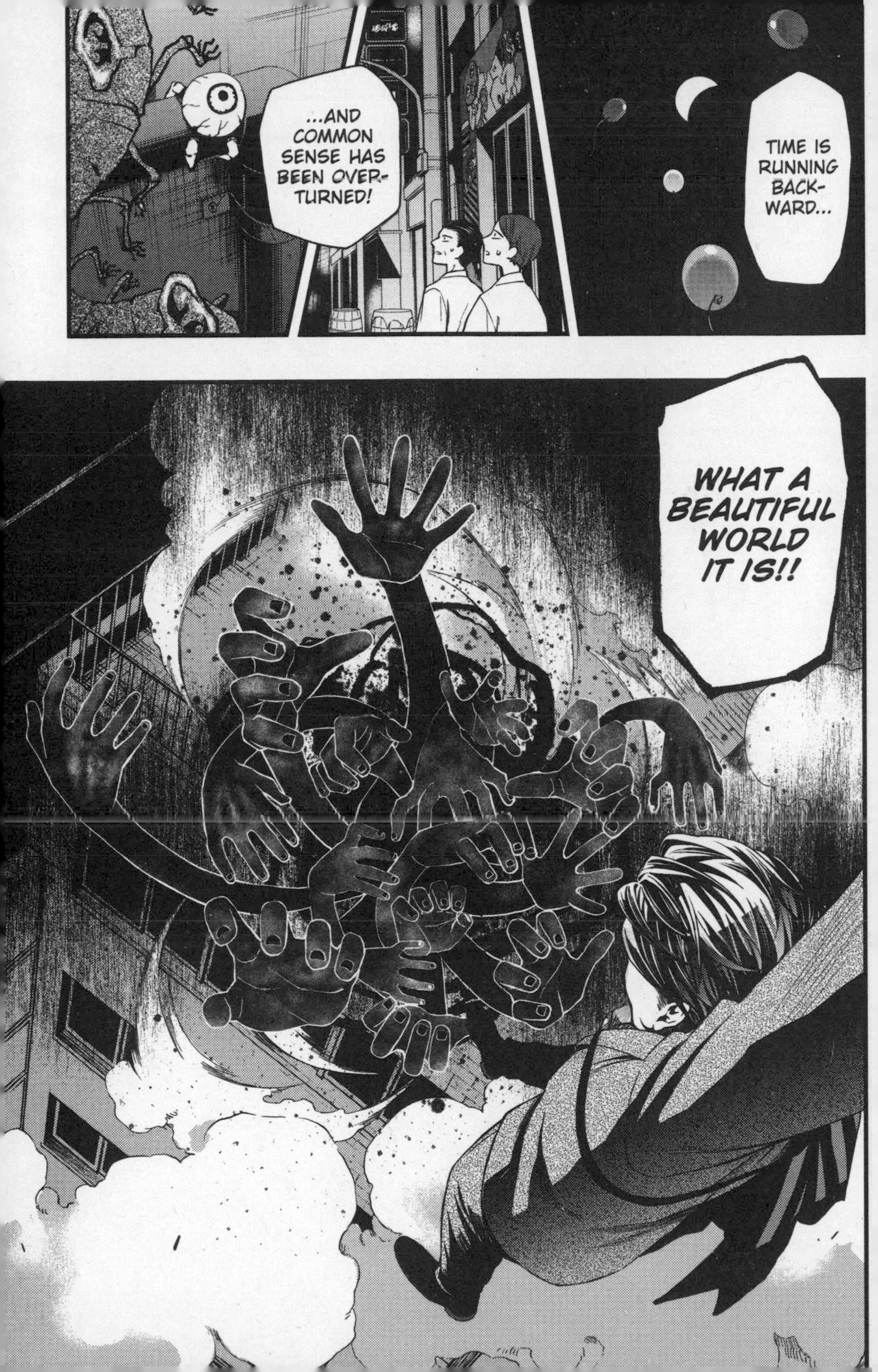
TIME IS RUNNING BACKWARD...
...AND COMMON SENSE HAS BEEN OVERTURNED!
WHAT A BEAUTIFUL WORLD IT IS!!

...MEANS SHARING YOUR SENSES WITH THE DEAD.

"SYMPATHIZING WITH THE SPIRITS OF THE DEAD"...

YOU "SAW" A FIELD OF WHEAT?

WHAT?

YOU CAN USE CRYSTAL BALLS LIKE THIS TO EXPERIENCE FOR YOURSELF THE SENSES OF SPIRITS THAT ARE FAR, FAR AWAY......

...YOUR SOUL DOESN'T SEEM TO HAVE BEEN ERODED.

AND YOU COULD SMELL THE WHEAT AND HEAR THE BREEZE?

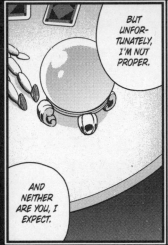

BUT UNFOR-TUNATELY, I'M NOT PROPER.

AND NEITHER ARE YOU, I EXPECT.

BIKU
(PLINCH)

ビク...

IF WE WERE IN A PROPER MASTER-PUPIL RELATIONSHIP, I'D TELL YOU, "DON'T SYMPATHIZE DIRECTLY! IT'S DANGEROUS!" AND GIVE YOU A SMACK.

INTRIGU-ING.

THAT WAY, THE POWER OF SYMPATHIZING WITH THE SPIRITS OF THE DEAD CAN BECOME A FORMIDABLE WEAPON FOR YOU.

LET'S TAKE SOME TIME TO THOROUGHLY TRAIN YOU IN THE ART OF PROTECTING YOUR SOUL.

ZUZU
(ZLOOSH)

ズ

ズ

AND THE SENSE OF TOUCH TOO. YOU SHOULD COME TO BE ABLE TO SHARE ALL OF YOUR SENSES WITH THE SPIRITS OF THE DEAD.

SIGHT, SMELL, HEARING, TASTE...

HOWEVER, THE ACTUAL APPLICATION OF THE TECHNIQUE CAN BE DIFFICULT.

WITHIN THE CONFINES OF THE BARRIER, YOU CAN DRAIN THE MAGICAL ESSENCE OF THE AREA TO ITS ABSOLUTE LIMIT......

BUT UNDER NORMAL CONDITIONS, YOU'LL BE BLOCKED BY THE SURROUNDING MAGICAL ESSENCE AND ACCOMPLISH LITTLE.

BUT SINCE COMING TO THIS WORLD, WHERE MAGICAL ESSENCE IS SO DILLUTED, HE CAN NOW DO SO TOTALLY AND WITHOUT LIMIT.

IN THE WORLD HE CAME FROM, THE CORPSE GOD WOULD SHARE HIS SENSE OF TOUCH WITH THE HANDS OF SPIRITS, IMPEDED THOUGH THEY WERE BY AN ATMOSPHERE RICH WITH MAGICAL ESSENCE.

...HE CREATED A LOOPHOLE THAT ALLOWS HIM TO USE THE EARTH'S OWN ENVIRONMENT AGAINST ITSELF WITHOUT EXPENDING TOO MUCH MAGIC.

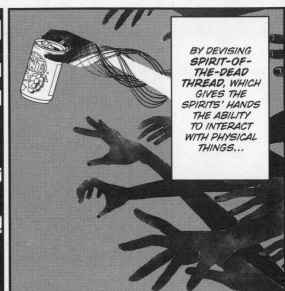

BY DEVISING SPIRIT-OF-THE-DEAD THREAD, WHICH GIVES THE SPIRITS' HANDS THE ABILITY TO INTERACT WITH PHYSICAL THINGS...

GO (WHOOSH)

EVENTUALLY, HIS FLOCK OF INVISIBLE HANDS WAS COMPLETE.

I STILL DON'T HAVE ENOUGH...

...TO KEEP DOWN LEMMINGS...

IN THAT CASE...I'LL FOCUS ON THE OTHER ONE...

ARE THEY ONE AND THE SAME? DO YOU HOLD THAT SECRET?

THE BONES FROM THAT BUILDING FIRE! AND THESE ARMS!

THE IMAGINARY MIDDLE SCHOOLER INSIDE ME IS JUMPING FOR JOY!!

PYON (HOP)

WE'LL MEET AGAIN!

AND I SWEAR I WILL GET TO THE BOTTOM OF ALL THIS.

BOFU (POOMF)

I SEE! DECEPTION HAS NO PLACE IN YOUR NAME!

ZUO (WHOOSH)

THE CORPSE GOD!

LEMMINGS.

...I NEVER WANT TO SEE YOU AGAIN IF I CAN HELP IT.

HYUOOO ZWOOOSH

PHEW.

......

BUT I'VE CAUGHT THE ONE WHO WAS DOWN BELOW.

DID HE GET AWAY?

THE ONE ON THE ROOF, YES.

220

: No mistake.

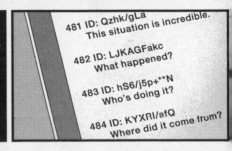

481 ID: Qzhk/gLa
This situation is incredible.

482 ID: LJKAGFakc
What happened?

483 ID: hS6/j5p+**N
Who's doing it?

484 ID: KYXRI/afQ
Where did it come from?

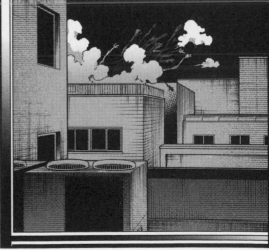

IT'S ONE OF THE POWERS OF OLD, PASSED DOWN THROUGH TIME.

DIVINE ARTS.

NECROMANCY.

SPIRIT CHANNELING.

THE SECRET ARTS OF THE ANCIENT COUNTRY FAR, FAR AWAY THAT NOT EVEN OUR ANCESTORS COULD HANDLE.

THE POWER THAT WILL GUIDE US TO THE NEXT LEVEL.

THE LOST POWER.

WE MUST HAVE IT.

WE MUST CONTROL IT.

IT IS OUR RIGHT.

OUR DUTY.

FIND IT.

FIND IT.

FIND IT.

HUNT IT DOWN.

SEARCH FOR IT.

TRACK IT DOWN.

SCOUR THE LAND.

Understood, comrades.
I will use the full extent of my resources.
Done properly, all our problems will be solved at the same time.

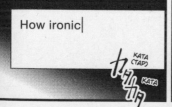

How ironic

KATA (TAP)

KATA

How ironic that the building where Hosorogi was disposed of would be where those carrying on his will are now gathering.

YOU CAN GIVE ME THE FULL DETAILS IN PERSON.

I SEE. UNDER- STOOD.

ANYWAY, TRY TO CATCH HIM IN THE ACT, YATSU.

...THIS TOWN'S ALWAYS BEEN A ROWDY PLACE, BUT...

IT LOOKS LIKE THE POLICE ARE ON THE MOVE.

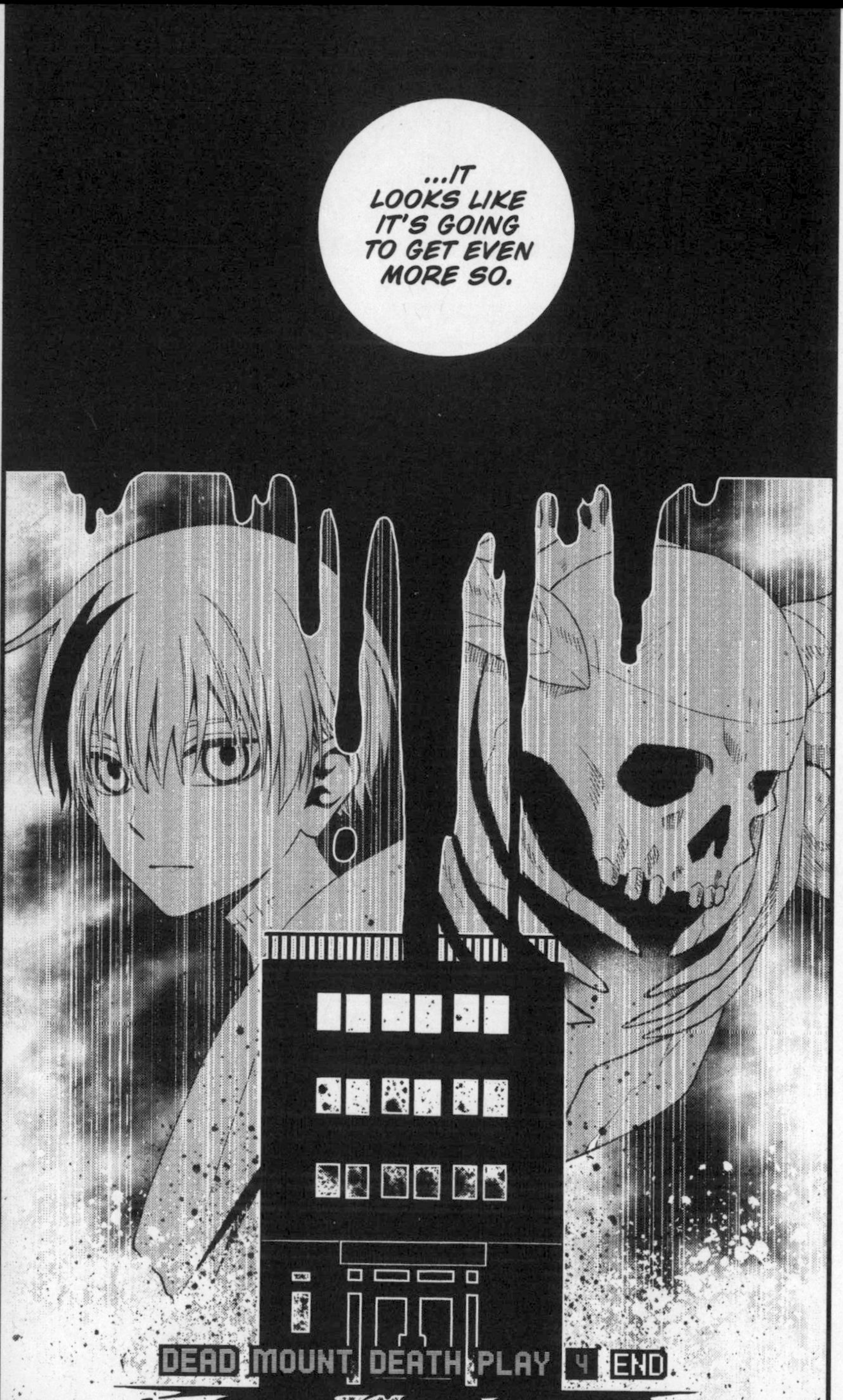
...IT LOOKS LIKE IT'S GOING TO GET EVEN MORE SO.
DEAD MOUNT DEATH PLAY 4 END

TRANSLATION NOTES

COMMON HONORIFICS

no honorific: Indicates familiarity or closeness; if used without permission or reason, addressing someone in this manner would constitute an insult.

-san: The Japanese equivalent of Mr./Mrs./Miss. If a situation calls for politeness, this is the fail-safe honorific.

-sama: Conveys great respect; may also indicate the social status of the speaker is lower than that of the addressee.

-kun: Used most often when referring to boys, this indicates affection or familiarity. Occasionally use by older men among their peers, but it may also be used by anyone referring to a person of lower standing.

-chan: An affectionate honorific indicating familiarity used mostly in reference to girls; also used in reference to cute persons or animals of either gender.

-senpai: A suffix used to address upperclassmen or more experienced coworkers.

-sensei: A respectful term for teachers, artists, or high-level professionals.

Currency Conversion
While conversaion rates fluctuate, an easy estimate for Japanese yen conversiaon is ¥100 to 1 USD.

Page 78
"Cool Biz" is a campaign started by the Japanese Ministry of the Environment to help reduce electricity consumption in Japan during summers by promoting a more relaxed dress code in offices.

Page 124
The fiend with twenty faces is a fictional character who serves as a recurring antagonist for dectective Akechi Kogoro in Ranpo Edogawa's mystery fiction.

Page 128
Bug's chant comes from a Japanese children's game in which one player is blindfolded while the other children join hands and walk in circles around while chanting the song. When the song stops, the blindfolded player tries to name the person standing directly behind them.

Page 207
Solitaire's salutation, **"Até breve, obrigado"** is Portugese for "See you soon, and thanks," though he seems to have forgotten it in the moment.

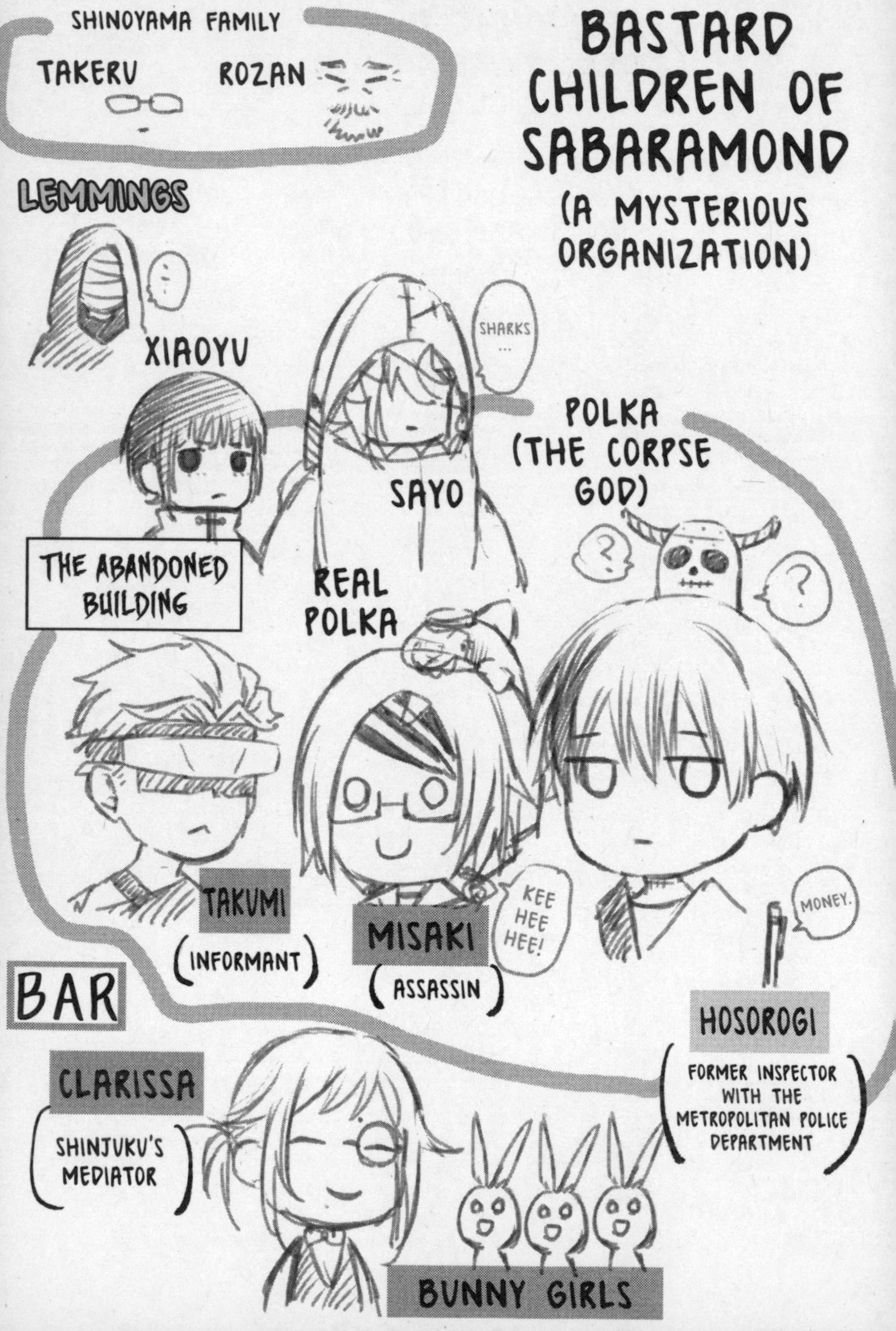
BASTARD CHILDREN OF SABARAMOND
(A MYSTERIOUS ORGANIZATION)
SHINOYAMA FAMILY
TAKERU
ROZAN
LEMMINGS
XIAOYU
SHARKS ...
SAYO
POLKA (THE CORPSE GOD)
THE ABANDONED BUILDING
REAL POLKA
TAKUMI
(INFORMANT)
MISAKI
(ASSASSIN)
KEE HEE HEE!
MONEY.
HOSOROGI
FORMER INSPECTOR WITH THE METROPOLITAN POLICE DEPARTMENT
BAR
CLARISSA
SHINJUKU'S MEDIATOR
BUNNY GIRLS

Super-Fun Illustrated Guide to
DEAD MOUNT DEATH PLAY

CHARACTER SUMMARY

ALTERNATE UNIVERSE: IMPERIAL COURT SORCERERS
FIRST RANK: ARIUS SABARAMOND
SECOND RANK: IZLIZ SWORDFLAIL
THIRD RANK: "UTSUROJUZA"
FOURTH RANK: "THE CORPSE GOD"

SMIRK

JIROTAROV
(SUPERINTENDENT GENERAL)

HABAKI
(SENIOR COMMISSIONER)

YAMADA-SAN

IN JAIL

THE GROCER

THE IMAGINARY MIDDLE SCHOOLER INSIDE ME IS CALLING...

SOLITAIRE

POLICE

COMPS-3

IWANOME

ARASE

YATSU

TOZAWA

AIKAWA

FIRE-BREATHING BUG

SPECIAL THANKS

WRITER:
RYOHGO NARITA

EDITOR:
KAZUHIDE SHIMIZU

TRANSLATION HELP:
MASAAKI SHIMIZU
JUYOUN LEE (YEN PRESS)

MAGIC RESEARCH:
KIYOMUNE MIWA (TEAM BARREL ROLL)

STAFF:
YOSHICHIKA EGUCHI
NORA
OTO
NANAMI HASAMA

Turn to the back of the book to read an exclusive bonus short story by Ryohgo Narita!

DEAD MOUNT DEATH PLAY

Episode ❹: The Storage Attack

Another arrives to sneer at Shinjuku.

DEAD MOUNT DEATH PLAY

TSK, TSK.

The Corpse God loses control, employing a technique from a distant alternate universe and leaving clear scratches on "the real world." Polka's memories of his "previous life" in the empire have attracted the attention of the "Bastard Children of Sabaramond." The two worlds are coming together, inviting unwelcome visitors. And everyone's lives heat up in Shinjuku......

...YOU MEAN THAT GRAFFITI? IT WAS THERE BEFORE WE MOVED IN.

SINCE IT TOOK SO LITTLE TO DIG UP THE INFORMATION, I DIDN'T THINK YOU WERE TRYING TO HIDE IT.

OH, I'M SORRY.

FORTU- NATELY IT ...N'T WASH ...WHAT OUT IT?

TO BE CONTINUED.........

DEAD MOUNT DEATH PLAY

4

STORY: **Ryohgo Narita**   ART: **Shinta Fujimoto**

Translation: Christine Dashiell * Lettering: Abigail Blackman

DEAD MOUNT DEATH PLAY Volume 4 © 2019 Ryohgo Narita, Shinta Fujimoto/SQUARE ENIX CO., LTD. First published in Japan in 2019 by SQUARE ENIX CO., LTD. English translation rights arranged with SQUARE ENIX CO., LTD. and Yen Press, LLC through Tuttle-Mori Agency, Inc., Tokyo.

English translation © 2020 by SQUARE ENIX CO., LTD.

Yen Press
150 West 30th Street, 19th Floor
New York, NY 10001

Visit us at yenpress.com
facebook.com/yenpress
twitter.com/yenpress
yenpress.tumblr.com
instagram.com/yenpress

First Yen Press eBook Edition: June 2020
The chapters in this volume were originally published as ebooks by Yen Press.

Yen Press is an imprint of Yen Press, LLC.
The Yen Press name and logo are trademarks of Yen Press, LLC.

The publisher is not responsible for websites (or their content) that are not owned by the publisher.

Library of Congress Control Number: 2018953479

ISBNs: 978-1-9753-1373-9 (paperback)
978-1-9753-1372-2 (ebook)

10 9 8 7 6 5 4 3 2 1

WOR

Printed in the United States of America

From beneath her animal-skull mask, Izliz seemed to give off a wry smile, but...

A voice disrupted the moment, echoing from far up in the sky:

"You said it."

"!?"

Shagrua's instincts put his entire body immediately on high alert.

Rather than his brain working out the identity of the voice, all the nerves running throughout his body and his soul remembered.

"I thought I sensed a nostalgic soul here in the ruined capital of the empire...... So it was you, the Calamity Crusher."

The "telepathic voice" pealed through him as though it had directly infiltrated his brain, and Shagrua recognized where he'd heard it.

Just then, "it" swooped down before his eyes, and he saw and knew for sure.

It was a dragon he himself had fought many years ago.

The being who had put Nyanild in a crisis years ago, known as the Late Emperor Killer.

"The Poisonous Dragon of Destruction......Pirawizzo......!"

And so, the gears of the world started turning.

On Byandy Peninsula, situated to the southwest of the empire, and in the ruined village at the borderlands to the northeast.

Though far, far away from one another, the cogs that were meant to never meet...did.

"……The pain's gone. Did you treat my wounds?"

"If you want to thank anybody, thank the tree branches around this bedroom. She's the one who administered the panacea tree sap to you."

"I see…… Thank you," Shagrua said, bowing his head to the tree branch reaching in through the window.

The branch quivered, and a flustered voice could be heard from the surrounding forest, yelping "Huh?!"

Ignoring that, Shagrua then thanked Izliz.

"I don't know why you did it, but you have my thanks for healing me."

"And yet, you're wary of me. Then again, you're right to be so."

"……I'm sorry. I don't mean to be, but I'm still conflicted. What I know about you and what the current situation presents just don't line up."

"Aww, what's the matter? Had you heard that I had annihilated an enemy army all by myself?"

Izliz had spoken in a manner of provocation, and after a moment's hesitation, Shagrua answered honestly.

"……I've heard tales that you filled the ruined country with zombies and deceived surrounding countries to make them think the nation was still alive and well…… Those kinds of stories."

With that, the voice of the "forest" once again sounded. "Of all the ridiculous—! That is absolutely and utterly without a doubt pure lies! That's—!"

"I don't care, Romelka. Once you start talking, you go on for too long, and I won't have it."

"Hmph! But,,, But,,,,,,!"

The "forest" tried to say more, but Izliz cut her off and then declared to Shagrua in a dignified tone, "No matter. I saved you on a whim. If you've developed a crush on me over it, then you can say so. After playing with you for three days, I'll just toss you out like yesterday's garbage."

Izliz's words sounded like teasing, but Shagrua answered in all seriousness. "I'm sorry, but I'm not the kind of dog who'd declare his love for someone he's only just met."

Then Shagrua shifted his gaze slightly downward and muttered half to himself, "Besides… Maybe my heart already belongs to another. Though, I doubt I'll ever see her again……"

"Well, well. What a straightlaced, sweet little boy we have here."

Recuria was on her guard as the boy walked toward her, but with a faint smile, he said to her, "Aww, don't worry, okay? I stored the gushing water in the area down below. Pani told me not to mess up any innocent third parties, see? Then again, any soldiers who survived the fall off the mountain will probably get eaten up by Radiall's pet anyway. Ha-ha! Poor guys, huh?"

The boy spoke all this with an indifferent air.

Recuria wasn't sure what to say to him, but in light of how things had gone so far, she mustered up her strength and said, "First off, thank you. For saving my life…… And allow me to introduce myself. I am Recuria Lofilardo. And you are?"

"Huh? I already know who you are, so you didn't have to waste your breath."

Giving two short laughs, the tattoo-faced boy shrugged and continued to speak while giving a polite bow.

"My name is Shula Zoozolozo Cramplamp Lampton. I'm an ally of the alchemist Pani, and I've come here as your special envoy. Nice to meet you." After this declaration, delivered with a theatrical flair, he put on a mischievous grin and added, "I'm the former third-ranking Imperial Court Sorcerer of the Empire of Byandy, Utsurojuza…… I'm sure I'm much better known by that name, eh?"

■ ■ ■

Byandy Peninsula

When Shagrua woke up, he found himself lying in a simple bed.

"Ah! You're awake, are you? Hold on tight. I was just speaking to Izliz on the beach, so I'll call her lickety-split in no time at all, sorry!" The voice was coming from a branch he could just spy through the crumbling roof and walls. From the looks of it, the building appeared to be deep in the forest.

In light of his current situation, Shagrua came to the conclusion that he must have been brought here as a prisoner of war.

"I was taken……alive……?"

Minutes later, as the "forest" had said, Izliz came in.

"Ah, I see you're awake. The Calamity Crusher boy. How do you feel?"

The voice continued to speak in an excited manner... And it seemed to Recuria to belong to a man as it candidly directed praise at her.

"Little priestess, you won the fight through perseverance. You might think this was a windfall, but you won this glory through your own efforts. Whoo-hoo! Super-impressive!"

"Windfall......? Who on earth......are you?"

While Recuria was bewildered, Domdaal swung his battle-ax as he yelled, "Hey! Where are you?! Don't hide! Show yourse—!"

But his words were cut off. A cold sweat sprang up all over Domdaal's body, and his face went white.

Before Domdaal knew it..."he" had appeared behind him.

"Didn't I tell you......to shut up?"

At first glance, he appeared to be an androgynous, beautiful boy with facial tattoos, but Recuria knew at once what he really was.

The quality of the aura surrounding the man was without a doubt human, but the rich vitality of his life suggested that this being already deviated from what one could call a human.

The boy was tapping Domdaal's back slowly with a finger.

"I don't know this Shagrua guy, so I don't care. But blaming the Corpse God for crimes he didn't commit? That's no good. You're lucky it was I who overheard you. If it'd been that old hag Izliz, she'd have probably put you through a thousand-year-long death. I like to get things over with quickly. Isn't that nice of me? Eh? Well?"

His words and actions seemed like empty threats, but with every touch of his finger, Domdaal's pale face was wrung with anguish and despair.

Then the boy slowly stepped away from Domdaal, and walking toward Recuria, he called back over his shoulder, "Why don't you just die already? Come on. Die—die. Die!"

His tone sounded as though he were shooing away a stray dog, and he held one hand up in the air. At that very second, a black pit suddenly opened in the air next to Domdaal, and the big man's organs shot out from within, blowing his own body away with the force of them.

Smeared in his own viscera, Domdaal was already dead, and he stared up at the sky with vacant eyes.

"Huh?"

"?! Wh-what the hell is this?!"

Washed out of the abandoned village halfway up the mountain, the soldiers tumbled down all the way into the valley.

The abandoned buildings, too, were wrenched from their foundations and carried off by the water, so that all who remained in the ruins of the village were Recuria, Domdaal, and Recuria's comrades protected within her defensive force field.

Recuria's eyes went wide at the sudden development she'd witnessed, and even Domdaal was looking around in confusion.

That's when...a voice sounded from nowhere in particular.

"Aww, we can't have that, see? It's no good. Would you please stop disparaging the Corpse God like that?"

"Wh...? Who are you?!"

At Domdaal's shout, a somewhat derisive laugh echoed from the surrounding air itself.

"Excuse me? You're asking me who I am? When asking someone for their name, don't you know you're supposed to offer your own first? But don't worry. I'll have you know I already know your name is Domdaal, based on that earlier conversation. And I have absolutely no interest in knowing anything about you beyond that. So you know what that means, right? Yep...... Shut up."

Only the last part was dipped in serious warning, as though the voice wanted to make it clear it had no interest whatsoever in the man called Domdaal.

Turning next to speak to Recuria, in contrast, the voice echoed with a somewhat friendly tone.

"I was thinking I'd just watch quietly and see who won at the very end, but you know what? I just couldn't help it when he started saying all those horrible things about my adorable little friend. Not to mention I've been searching for you anyway because I have some business with you; so when it looked like you were going to die, I thought I might as well store you."

the soldiers unlucky enough to be caught in his path against the wall of an abandoned house.

"......That man, too, was initially all on his own."

With a face of sorrow, Recuria once again fell to her knees.

But she was not satisfied merely having defeated the ringleader.

In the few seconds before the surrounding soldiers could get back into formation, she readied her body's magic. She figured if she could hammer a psychological manipulation-type technique into their heads while they were still disoriented, she could knock them out and probably escape.

Now that she had vanquished Domdaal who had been clad in armor with multiple layers of protection, it was more than possible.

Making up her mind, Recuria kept up her guard as she concentrated her senses...

"That surprised me......"

"!"

Rubble from the dilapidated building gave way, and Domdaal stood, throwing the unconscious bodies of soldiers away from him with one hand.

"You were able to damage my armor, and after I'd been told that it could block even the fangs of a dragon...... As far as magic goes, what you have probably surpasses even Shagrua, don't you agree......?"

He picked up the giant battle-ax that had fallen to the ground in one hand and, hefting it onto his shoulder, approached Recuria.

"Don't worry. I'll tell them that, in your pursuit of the fugitive Shagrua, you were killed by the Corpse God who had possessed his body....... That's the story I'll give them in my report."

"......!"

"If you don't like it, then you can take it up with the mad Shagrua and the Corpse God!"

Giving an exceptionally hateful laugh, Domdaal swung his ax.

Hoping to convert her own life force into one last magical attack, Recuria held her hand over her heart, when—

Suddenly, a cold, muddy stream sprang forth and gushed down from the sky, washing away the surrounding soldiers with a tremendous force.

"......I see. So not only did the higher-ups instigate this, but your own personal ego has gotten involved."

"Say what you like. You should have stayed like how Shagrua was before he absconded: a weapon who only hunted divine enemies without questioning things. This is what you get for acquiring knowledge and a chivalrous spirit you had no business acquiring."

His contentious words were meant to break Recuria's as of yet unbroken spirit. But...

Not only did they fail to break her spirit, they ended up setting alight a blaze in her eyes.

"......Take that back."

"Excuse me?"

"That man is not a weapon."

"......Ha! You're right! He's not a weapon after all. He's a downright monster who was born with the Evil Eye! That's why he became a divine enemy in the end!"

As Domdaal gave a derisive laugh, Recuria regarded him with open hostility, and, though already at her limit, she rose to her feet, her body trembling.

"How dare you......claim you speak the words of god?"

"What are you going to do about it? With how greatly we outnumber you, you think you can turn the tables all on your own? Don't you agree this situation is more than adequate an excuse for you to give up and plead for your life?" Domdaal said, provoking her even further.

But Recuria answered with only a slightly sad smile.

"That......is no excuse."

In that instant, magic swelled up from her feet. The veins and muscle fibers of her legs, which were fortified beyond their limit with the aid of physical strengthening, shredded as they launched her body at Domdaal like a cannon.

"What the......?!"

She plunged the stick she held in her hand into the junction at the neck of his armored suit and ran the majority of her remaining magic into its tip.

An explosion rocked the air, and the suit of armor's helmet flew off.

Domdaal's substantial bulk was also blown back, and he pinned some of

they did the actual teachings of the Church and, in particular, were thought to have a big influence on others.

Recuria herself had at one time marked them as the kind of exceptional humans needed to clear Shagrua's name, so she realized right away the commonality between the gathered members.

As a result…with no time to plan a countermeasure, they were pounced upon and attacked in that abandoned village they had convened in.

"Oh, bother. I tried asking a leading question to see how much you know, but……I guess you really don't know anything. Or maybe you're only feigning ignorance……"

The big man in front of Recuria, Lord Domdaal, was rumored to be an enforcer with the Church.

If Shagrua was a hero who took on substantial "individuals" like dragons and devils, then this man was a bold and daring man who specialized in quelling "masses" such as armored heretical groups and hordes of monsters.

But the truth of the matter was that he was related to the kingdom's aristocracy who were granted stable positions in exchange for doing the Church's "dirty work." And he was the man who orchestrated a variety of disruptive maneuvers to keep Shagrua's influence from spreading to the political realm of the kingdom.

"You were too close to Shagrua."

An overwhelming number had attacked the followers of the Calamity Crusher now gathered in the abandoned village.

Forced to take the defensive against a military strength ten times greater than their own, one by one they fell until the only defender left standing and in one piece was Recuria.

As though deciding she was already beaten, all the surrounding soldiers relaxed as sneers came to their lips.

Their faces looked like they couldn't wait to see how Domdaal would punish the priestess ranked too high above them to touch.

As though answering the expectations of his men, Domdaal raised his voice. "Recuria, your impressive efforts have won you achievements as of late, but……we can't have someone who distrusts the Church's upper echelons wielding too much influence."

"......Did you act on your own authority, Lord Domdaal?"

"Don't give me attitude. You should be able to at least guess who instigated all this."

"No. If I may be so blunt...... There are too many suspicious higher-ups in the Church to know for sure."

Head Priestess Recuria.

She was a holy practitioner who had long assisted Shagrua and accompanied him on many dangerous missions with the mastery of her techniques.

After hearing Shagrua's final words just before he went missing, Recuria had become like a different person. She made every effort to band the bewildered clergymen together into a troupe that would march under a different banner.

She was a master not of the lead holy arts of the Geldwood Church that dealt with spiritual intervention, but the branch that mainly focused on physical healing and revitalization as well as fortifying weapons. However, having walked with the hero known as Shagrua for so long, hers was a power considered at the top of the class within the religious organization, leading her into fresh territory that even included tactics for taking on "divine enemies."

However, in doing so, there came to be people who were displeased with her starting to win over the hearts of the people and priest soldiers as the "successor of Shagrua."

One might say her current situation was a testament to their veiled resentment.

Recuria had brought a number of trustworthy subordinates with her to these borderlands after receiving an order from the Church authorities to "perform an investigation in pursuit of bringing Shagrua to justice" based on information that Shagrua had gone into hiding here.

Recuria guessed that the information was leading her into a trap, but she still didn't have the power to overtly object to orders from above.

Her hunch changed to certainty when the faces she met at the site were very familiar.

They were priest soldiers who believed more in "the hero Shagrua" than

Though a wide variety of rumors flew about, they always arrived at the same conclusion:

They said as soon as he was found...he would have to be put down.

True, the majority of the Church's clergymen and priest soldiers regarded Shagrua as a hero.

There were also many who couldn't believe he deserved such a punishment, but the fact that he had almost killed a number of the nineteen highest-ranking religious leaders of the Church weighed heavily on the minds of those pious followers.

In time, with members of the Church's upper echelon shrewdly manipulating information, people stopped calling the hero by his nickname, the Calamity Crusher. People now acknowledged him as Calamity.

Except for one. A priestess who had fought alongside the Calamity Crusher longer than anybody.

■■■

Kingdom of Nyanild, along the northeastern border

"......You've given us a lot of trouble, Recuria."

The speaker was a large and extremely tall man carrying a battle-ax and entirely clad in heavy armor. His armor was cast with several layers of "protection" and indicated he was a Geldwood Church soldier.

Surprisingly enough, however, the person kneeling before him...was a young woman who wore the priestess robes of the same Geldwood Church.

She had erected a force field using holy runes, and close to ten wounded and fallen soldiers lay behind her. What now surrounded the wounded troupe was a band of nearly a hundred men also clad in the same Geldwood Church armor.

Caught in an apparent case of infighting, the priestess soldier named Recuria glared up at the large man with flashing eyes, ignoring the hopelessness of her position.

DEAD MOUNT DEATH PLAY

Episode ❹: The Storage Attack

by Ryohgo Narita

Manga exclusive bonus short story

The Calamity Crusher, Shagrua, had absconded from the kingdom.

The story was kept a secret from the populace by the authorities, but no small tremor ran through the holy practitioners and priests of the Church as all manner of rumor, containing both fact and fiction, hung like a spreading haze over them.

They said the Calamity Crusher had died.

They said the hero Shagrua's flesh had been lost to evil spirits.

They said the soul of the Corpse God, whom he was supposed to have defeated, had in fact taken over the body of that strongest of men.

They said he had thrashed a number of senior church officials and then made off with valuable treasures and documents.

They said he was actually a spy with the northern Allied Powers.

They said there was no doubt he had been in league with the Corpse God from the very start.

They said Shagrua was already long dead from a battle in a coal mine.

They said, after that, Shagrua had been replaced by a golem made by the alchemist Pani.

They said, no, all along he was a dragon who had taken the form of a human.

They said, they said, they said…